# Matcha
## A Lifestyle Guide

**By Jessica Flint and Anna Kavaliunas**

**Recipes by Ben Mims**

**Photography by Scott Gordon Bleicher**

DOVETAIL

# Table of Contents

# *Introduction*

This isn't your typical girl-meets-matcha story. That's because there is no typical girl-meets-matcha story. Before we set out to write this book, we thought we were a pretty big deal when it came to powdered green tea. We live in New York City, and every Saturday after our workouts, we would meet at Chalait, our favorite matcha bar, which at the time was located in the West Village. We'd strategically maneuver our way through throngs of patrons who were snapping photos of their neon-green lattes and avocado toasts so we could secure our coveted seats at the bar (and eavesdrop on awful first dates). We'd sit there for hours, literally.

We were both at interesting points in our lives. Jess had just moved in with her boyfriend and was detoxifying her life, including a transition to using all-natural beauty products (a harder task than you'd think). Anna had just returned from a stint in Los Angeles and was a recovering pretentious hippie adjusting back to the frenetic pace of Manhattan, one more almond milk cortado and one less blonde ecaille highlight at a time.

We were past our "going crazy in New York" years (minus that one raw oyster bar incident), both incredibly focused on our health and wellness. Instead of grabbing a glass of wine to shoot the shit after our workouts, we went for matcha, at first because Anna was missing the buttery matcha latte from the West Coast health-food mecca Erewhon. As our Saturday ritual became more established, the more we looked forward to it. We like to think that the matcha deepened our conversations as we collectively found solutions for problems and laughed more than either of us had in a while.

Our lives ebbed and flowed throughout this period—from lost relationships and exhausting health issues to empowering breakups with boutique gyms, new hair colors, and the exciting, joint adventure of climbing Kilimanjaro—but we made it a point to meet once a week no matter what, to simply enjoy some damn good matcha. Without knowing it, we were truly embodying

the spiritual and physical effects of the drink: calming and focusing our lives through the simple act of making tea. (Okay, watching Chalait matcharista John make our tea.)

As time went on, we got the gist of matcha—the history, the health benefits, and, most importantly, the deliciousness of the creamy almond-milk matcha latte hitting our lips. One sunny and sweaty New York afternoon, less than a year into our matcha Saturdays, we came to the realization that we had lost our creativity—not just in writing, but in bringing more joyful and fun experiences into our lives. We decided to turn our matcha time into a sort of workshop, using it to bounce ideas off each other, revisit long lost projects and develop new ones, and set goals and dreams for the future. Jess brought her practicality; Anna brought her imagination. We blended together like the sweet umami of the matcha.

The next weekend we started writing this book.

# Chapter 1
# What is Matcha?

## Matcha 101

Karlie Kloss isn't just a model: she's a supermodel. This book isn't just about green tea: it's about matcha. Gwyneth Paltrow has blogged about it. Millennials populate Instagram with it. Catwalkers get through Fashion Week on it. Finance guys take midday breaks to fist-bump over $6 shots of it. ("Cool *koicha*, bro!") Silicon Valley entrepreneurs do DEFCON levels of it. Beauty influencers...bathe in it. These days it seems like matcha is both everywhere and yet not readily available anywhere, which is fitting considering it's a powder of contradictions, an elixir that carries with it an air of mythical allure and intimidation.

But if that's all there was to matcha, you wouldn't be reading a whole book about it. The tea's newfound cult reflects the current zeitgeist in America: it epitomizes health and wellness, creates the perfect balance between epicureanism and aesthetics, thrives on social media, and feeds off of a culture striving to be superhuman. Though matcha isn't new, its roots and ritual actually reach back some five thousand years to Asia. So how did something so antiquated only now become so hot? And more importantly—unlike the cronut or maple water—why will the matcha trend last?

We'll get into all of this, but first, let's discuss matcha basics.

## Matcha Is a Green Tea

If you already knew that, you get a gold—no, a green—sticker. Most tea leaves—loose leaf and those found in everyday tea bags of all varieties (green, black, white, oolong, Pu-erh)—are steeped in water to extract their flavor and benefits. Matcha, however, is the whole tea leaf ground into a powder and consumed. Simply put, when matcha is added to water or milk, you are literally drinking a plant. Or eating it: Mix matcha with black pepper and pink salt and sprinkle it over eggs, salmon, or steak; use it in savory dishes, such as matcha pasta, shaved

broccoli salad, or vegan cashew soup; bake with it—think carrot cake, shortbread and cookies—and sift it over vanilla ice cream. And yes, cocktails! In other words, it's a versatile pantry item.

## It's Sourced from Japan

Just like real Champagne comes from France's Champagne region and bona fide Kampot pepper comes from Kampot, Cambodia, authentic matcha comes from Japan. No one argues with the fact that the top matcha is from Japan. The region best known for its matcha is Uji, located on the outskirts of Kyoto, Japan's cultural capital, which is about 280 miles southwest of Tokyo, the country's political capital. Uji is the birthplace of matcha, the OG of Japanese tea. With matcha, all roads lead back to the farmers, and the ones in Uji have been growing and harvesting the tea for more than eight hundred years, passing down traditions through family lineages. There are other regions in Japan that also produce legit matcha, such as Nishio (about 100 miles east of Kyoto), and Fukuoka, on the southern island of Kyushu (about 400 miles south of Kyoto). Nishio is known for mass-producing matcha, whereas Fukuoka has a younger and hungrier entrepreneurial spirit, meaning there is more experimentation with methods that keep quality high but also produce enough tea to meet the demands of the modern world.

We are dubious about matcha from China, India, Taiwan, Thailand, Kenya, or elsewhere. Purchasing tea from anywhere but Japan is like buying a counterfeit Goyard handbag (unless it's a really good one... from Japan).

## Ask the Expert:

*What's it like developing a relationship with a Japanese matcha source?*

It took me three years before our matcha producer in Japan would sell to me. That's how they do business. They want to make sure they are partnering with a trusted network so that the product they work so hard on is getting the proper care. That means everything from packaging to storage to sales, and ensuring that the turnover is quick so the matcha isn't sitting around.

*How would you describe the flavor profiles of matcha from different regions?*

Uji's flavor is compelling because of the land and soil, what fertilizer they use, the varieties of leaves, and how they produce the tea. The matcha is ambrosial, floral, and a deep-green color because of very high chlorophyll levels. Matcha from Nishio is very light, pleasing, approachable, unassuming, and not the most complex or interesting. It's fresh and easy to drink. Fukuoka has more of an umami taste, buttery lasting creaminess, and toasty, chocolatey, and peanuty notes. Westerners like it. More often than not in blind tastings, we pick Fukuoka. It's less astringent, longer lasting. First-time matcha drinkers enjoy it. With more experience, Uji teas become easier to drink.

### Zach Mangan
*Kettl, New York City*

## Matcha Has Unique Characteristics

A tea is a tea is a tea. And Phil Collins is just some guy singing. All teas come from the same basic *Camellia sinensis* plant, but varietals can be differentiated by geography and growing and processing methods. There are several ways matcha distinguishes itself from regular green tea: it's a *tencha* leaf, meaning it's shade grown, which changes its color and nutrients; it's destemmed and deveined during processing, thereby altering its flavor; and, as you've already learned, matcha is ground into a fine powder.

Within the matcha family, there are two tea grades: ceremonial and culinary. Ceremonial matcha is generally whisked with water for drinking. The higher quality the tea, the sweeter and smoother it is. The cheaper culinary stuff is used for cooking and baking, where sugar and other ingredients can tame its bitterness; it's also used in some drinks with milk, which can accommodate bitterness, too.

## How It's Mixed Matters

Matcha's miniscule leaf particles are not water soluble, meaning they won't dissolve when added to water or milk. Instead, the powder needs to be suspended in liquid. This makes matcha the only suspension tea in the Japanese tea canon. Stirring it with a spoon will only make it clumpy. The bubbles formed by aerating the drink through whisking, shaking, or blending are what hold the powder in place and add the delightful frothiness on top. (It should look like a well-poured craft beer, not the residue of a Cancún foam party.) Because it's a suspension tea, if you let a matcha beverage sit for too long, the solids will settle at the bottom.

The preparation of matcha is very versatile. In Japan, it's traditionally made two ways: *usucha*, or "thin," and *koicha*, or "thick." Both types are served hot in a bowl called a *chawan*. *Usucha* uses a ratio of about 2 grams (1 teaspoon) of matcha to about 2 ounces (¼ cup) of water. *Koicha* uses a double serving of matcha and the same amount of water. The thick texture is more paint-like—kind of like that glue you ate as a child, but better tasting. And less weird.

In the United States, it's more common to drink matcha in a cup, hot or cold, with 2 grams of matcha blended with up to 12 ounces (1½ cups) of water or milk.

## *It Should Definitely Taste Good*

Matcha shouldn't be a challenge to drink. On a simplistic level, matcha mixed with water or milk will be creamy (like blended baby vegetables), heavy in umami (that satisfyingly savory fifth taste), and rich, even though there's no fat in it. Like oenophiles, matcha connoisseurs get off on the various aromas, flavors, textures, aftertastes, and food pairings. A sophisticated tea sommelier might describe matcha's flavor profile as "bittersweet dark-chocolate astringency meets freshly cut grass and spinach, perhaps with a hint of ocean, roasted corn, or seawater brininess." It should be smooth, with balance and complexity, and not bitter with a gritty texture; topped with a thick head; and devoid of baking soda-esque lumps at the bottom of the cup. The longer the finish, the better, too. In other words, anyone who's not a sophisticated tea sommelier can safely describe matcha as "good."

Bad matcha will be bitter and astringent, smelling like hay or burnt grass. Personally, we have never eaten hay or burnt grass, and we don't want to start now.

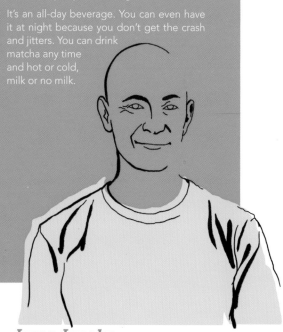

## Ask the Expert:

*Where do you buy your matcha from?*

Japan. It's actually gotten harder because of the demand. Sourcing it requires relationships built with integrity and trust. We commit to purchasing three years out. Yes, we buy futures on tea so we can guarantee we can get it and have the quality that we've always had.

*What is your favorite matcha flavor profile?*

I've been going for more umami-focused matchas recently. Some have a really wild flavor—like baked potatoes with butter.

*What's a typical evolution of a matcha drinker?*

They'll start with a matcha latte, which is how they learn about the origin of matcha. After they have the lattes for a while, then they say, "Let me try it straight. I want to taste the grassy notes and spinach." At that point they start to appreciate the level of craft with the whisking. But people bounce back and forth between the latte and drinking it straight.

*Is matcha just for mornings?*

It's an all-day beverage. You can even have it at night because you don't get the crash and jitters. You can drink matcha any time and hot or cold, milk or no milk.

### Jesse Jacobs
*Samovar Tea Bar, San Francisco*

## Naturally, Matcha is Healthy

Matcha's catechin polyphenols, or compound antioxidants, have been shown to protect against cancer, ward off cardiovascular disease, reduce cholesterol and blood pressure, detoxify the blood, alkalize the body, and stabilize blood sugars. A specific catechin polyphenol worth noting is epigallocatechin gallate (EGCG); matcha contains 140 times more of it compared to other green teas. EGCG amplifies the antioxidant activity in blood while increasing the body's ability to burn fat, promoting weight loss. The EGCG it contains is partly why matcha has about 10 times the nutrients and health benefits of regular green tea. (Also, remember that with matcha you consume the whole tea leaf, which means you receive more antioxidants than with steeped tea.) Did we mention that not all green teas are created equal? Believe it or not, there is actually a unit of measurement for antioxidants. It's called the oxygen radical absorbance capacity. Matcha's level is 1,440. That's more than four times the amount found in goji berries and dark chocolate, both of which are known for their high levels of antioxidants.

### Antioxidants (in grams)

| | |
|---|---|
| Matcha | 1,440 g |
| Goji berries | 253 g |
| Dark Chocolate | 227 g |
| Pecans | 180 g |
| Walnuts | 135 g |
| Pomegranate | 105 g |
| Wild Blueberries | 93 g |
| Açaí Berries | 55 g |
| Broccoli | 31 g |

## It's a Calming Stimulant

A 2-ounce serving of matcha contains about 70 milligrams of caffeine. This is about double the amount in a cup of regular green tea. Matcha contains up to 60 percent of the caffeine in espresso; 75 percent of that in a cup of coffee; and 80 percent of that in Red Bull (do people still drink this stuff?). Due to matcha's high amino acid content (specifically L-theanine, which we'll get to in a second), the caffeine in matcha enters your system more slowly than coffee. That equals no crash, no jitters. It's a smooth ride. If coffee is Guns 'N' Roses coursing through your veins, matcha is Hall & Oates. If anything, matcha is the alkalizing coffee, delivering energizing effects while being more gastrointestinally tolerable.

The other way matcha one-ups regular green tea is that matcha contains five times more L-theanine, a feel-good amino acid that stimulates the alpha brain waves that decrease stress. This effect is what the Japanese Buddhists call *satori*, a calm euphoria similar to that brought on by meditation. The slow-release caffeine combined with the L-theanine improves cognitive function while creating a more consistent, sustained energy. Matcha relaxes and energizes at the same time. We heard about a big-deal neurosurgeon who consumes it regularly, achieving alertness and focus without the jitters that would affect his hands during intense surgery—the same reason we drink it before putting on mascara.

## All This Means...

Matcha isn't just a trend. It's easy to see why it is becoming part of modern American culture: it's delicious, functional, provides unique health benefits, and it opens up a whole new world of flow-state energy in which you're riding a gentle calm but have mental clarity. On top of this, it's all-natural, which is even more mind-blowing. Where has matcha been all our lives? Now *this* is why you're reading a book on tea, of all things!

## Matcha Misconceptions

Googling "matcha" is like opening your door to a swindling (and hopefully good-looking) snake-oil salesman. You name it, it's got it! You've heard it, it's true! The search-engine rabbit hole can be as confusing as trying to figure out why models keep dating Harry Styles, even though they knew he was trouble when he walked in (#teamtaytay). Here are some of the biggest matcha myths debunked. Trust us.

*Fiction: Matcha is just green tea.*

Fact: It's the only green tea that uses the whole tea leaf, ground into a fine powder. It's a suspension tea that needs to be whisked or shaken with hot water versus being steeped.

*Fiction: Matcha can be produced anywhere.*

Fact: High-quality matcha is only from Japan. This could change in the future, but for now, it is what it is.

*Fiction: Just pour hot water over it and enjoy.*

Fact: Matcha doesn't dissolve in water, so you will enjoy some nice green clumps if this is all you do. Though finely ground, you still need to whisk or shake matcha to break it up.

*Fiction: Higher-quality matcha equals higher-quality food.*

Fact: Culinary matcha is lower grade on purpose because of its ability to adapt to other ingredients. That said, you can—and in many cases should—use higher-grade matcha in recipes (such as the ones that start on page 56), if you want the umami-rich flavor and vibrant-green color to shine through.

*Fiction: Matcha can be brewed like coffee.*
Fact: Just, no.

*Fiction: All powdered green tea is matcha.*

Fact: Matcha is the only powdered tea produced from *tencha*, a shade-grown leaf. It's a form of green tea, but not all green tea powder is matcha. Don't even get us started on white and black "matcha."

*Fiction: Matcha is absurdly expensive.*

Fact: Not really. It works out to about $1 a gram, and a typical serving is about 2 grams.

*Fiction: I have to use a bamboo whisk.*

Fact: If you want to be legit or impress people, then yes. Bamboo whisks look pretty cool. But at home, use a cocktail or other drink shaker, a handheld milk frother, or an electric blender.

*Fiction: If you drink matcha, you shouldn't drink coffee.*

Fact: Drinking matcha isn't cheating on coffee, nor is it beverage polygamy. They complement more than they compete. Those who appreciate the culture of coffee and the unique story of a single-origin roast should be equally enamored by the personal tapestry of each matcha blend.

*Fiction: Matcha is bitter.*

Fact: If you're under this impression, then you've only had really bad matcha. High-end matcha is pure umami.

# Chapter 2
# Matcha, Then and Now

## The Chinese Get It Started

Matcha's origins date back some five thousand years, which means a lot of the drink's history revolves around legends starring ancient Asian VIPs (think herbologists, monks, samurai warriors). The widely accepted story begins in southern China, where green tea is indigenous and where Shennong, the father of Chinese medicine, apparently first brewed it around 2700 BC. The Chinese grew to appreciate green tea for its medicinal properties, and Zen Buddhist monks got into it to stay awake during meditation so they could reach enlightenment (smart).

It wasn't until China's Tang Dynasty (618–907), however, that tea became trendy. This was thanks in large part to tea saint Lu Yü, who, sometime around the year 760, wrote a tea tell-all called *The Classic of Tea*. The book elevated the beverage to an art form and propelled Yü into early-millennia Kardashian-level fame. The guide provided how-tos on everything from growing the plant to selecting the leaves to brewing the drink. Regarding the latter, during the Tang Dynasty, the Chinese steamed and molded tea leaves into cakes for easy storage and transportation. Yü said cake-tea should be roasted until soft, shredded into a powder between fine pieces of paper, and added to hot water with salt; tea-ists followed suit.

But fads, as we know, come and go, and during China's Song Dynasty (960–1279) boiled tea fell out of favor. The new "it" beverage was whipped tea: steamed and dried tea leaves were ground by a stone mill, and the resulting powder was then mixed into hot water (sans salt) with a bamboo whisk and served in a bowl. The tea probably wasn't called matcha yet—the Japanese christened it that (*ma* is Japanese for "powder," and *ocha* means "tea")—but this new whipped tea set the stage for the rise of matcha as we know it today.

## The Japanese Perfect It

Due to some, shall we say, "leadership changes" in China beginning in the thirteenth century, whipped tea was eventually forgotten and replaced by steeped teas. The Japanese intelligentsia, on the other hand, couldn't get enough of the powdered green stuff. That's because matcha's inciting incident had occurred in 1191, when the Japanese Buddhist monk Myōan Eisai, who had received his Zen certification in China, returned home and brought the tea hype with him. In 1214, Eisai pulled a "Yü" and wrote a book called *How to Stay Healthy Drinking Tea*. It was a self-help tome of sorts (the first line reads, "Tea is the ultimate mental and medical remedy and has the ability to make one's life more full and complete.") that gained favor with Japan's elite, especially among the samurais, who saw tea as symbolic power. They also loved how tea gave them sustained energy and mental sharpness. It just so happens that around the same time that Eisai was waxing poetic about tea, Japanese farmers began growing it in Uji, just outside of Kyoto (Japan's capital until 1868, when

# The History of Matcha

**2700 BC**

Shennong, the father of Chinese medicine, brewed the first green tea, which was appreciated for its medicinal properties.

**618–907 AD**

China's Tang Dynasty made green tea trendy when tea saint Lu Yü wrote a tea tell-all called The Classic of Tea in 760.

**1214 AD**

China forgot about whipped tea, but the Japanese Buddhist monk Myōan Eisai increased its hype when he penned a book called How to Stay Healthy Drinking Tea.

**960–1279 AD**

Boiled tea fell out of favor and was replaced by whipped tea: steamed and dried leaves were ground by a stone mill into a powder that was mixed in hot water with a bamboo whisk.

**1579 AD**

Japanese Zen-master Sen No Rikyū popularized many aspects of the tea ceremony, known as the Way of Tea, that are still prevalent today in Japan.

**1738 AD**

Tea purveyor Soen Nagatani developed a new process of harvesting matcha called the "Uji method," which is more effective than roasting and drying tea leaves.

**Today**

After matcha became more accessible in Japan, it migrated to the United States, where beverages such as the matcha latte have made the powdered green tea a phenomenon.

**19th Century**

Japan began exporting tea in 1610. By the nineteenth century it was shipping 181 tons of green tea overseas per year, including to the United States.

## Ask the Expert:

*What's your top tip for a first-time matcha drinker?*

Think of the matcha shot as replacing the espresso shot. However you build your espresso drink is how you should build your matcha drink.

*Do you think that matcha's authenticity could be lost in the American matcha boom?*

At Chalait, we try to not add matcha to everything, but where it is appropriate and tastes good. People are taking the trend and using it everywhere, even if it's not complementary. Producing matcha is so labor intensive. It's someone going out to the fields, picking the teas themselves, and bringing it back. Every tin on the shelf is picked by a person. It isn't automated. It's made with love. So everything made with matcha needs to reflect that, too.

*Michelle Puyane*
Chalait, New York City

the emperor's home was moved to Tokyo). In the early days in Japan, powdered green tea was made from a raw tea called *sencha*. This type of tea leaf is grown uncovered in the sun from planting to picking. Today, 80 percent of Japan's tea is sencha. But at some point in the fifteenth or sixteenth century, the dawn of shade-grown tea plants occurred; approximately four weeks before the end of the harvest, usually in late April or early May, the tea fields were covered to prevent direct sunlight from hitting the plants.

Somebody all those many years ago figured out that shading the plant forces it to say, "Okay, I'm in trouble—I need to create energy." The plant starts to produce L-theanine as an alternate food source. The change in photosynthesis remixes the plant's internal chemistry, which affects its color and flavor in addition to its nutrients. In the early shade-grown days, farmers hammered bamboo poles around a tea field's perimeter and used crisscrossed hemp string to create a faux ceiling, which they'd cover with hay to force the plants to struggle to find light. Today, straw is still used, as are bamboo slats or black fabric.

## A Brief Note on the Tea Ceremony

Matcha's popularity rose in the sixteenth century in Japan due to the *chanoyu*, or the tea ceremony, which was introduced as a way for Japanese rulers, warriors, and merchants to be social. The so-called Way of Tea is a complex Japanese cultural activity that, at its most basic level, can be boiled down to a host serving tea to a guest. A traditional Japanese ceremony is a four-hour-long, mostly no-talking affair among a small group of people that celebrates the fact that there will never be another moment or encounter like the one happening at that instant. The focus is the interaction between the host, guests, and utensils (for more, see page 24).

It can take as many as twenty years to learn how to perfect the tea ceremony, which is a closed-off and secretive practice in which grand masters are treated like demigods. In many ways, the Way of Tea is a choreographed and disciplined self-improvement project. Those performing the ritual show their worth through grit: if they can study the ceremony for two decades—not necessarily a pleasant endeavor—they've proven to the world (and themselves) that they have the wherewithal to belong in the tea world. In other words, it's a marathon, not your neighborhood 5K Turkey Trot.

In the late sixteenth century, the Japanese Zen-master Sen No Rikyū popularized many aspects of the tea ceremony that are still prevalent today, such as finding beauty and simplicity in imperfection, known to the Japanese as *wabi sabi*. It is worth mentioning, however, that Rikyū is a little like Vincent van Gogh or F. Scott Fitzgerald: only after his death was he elevated to sacred icon status. Regardless, as Rikyū's version of the tea ceremony became the upper crust's preferred art form, matcha itself became more elitist. Matcha was very valuable, and only a small number of purveyors were allowed to make it. Meanwhile, the commoners were forced to drink *bancha*, a brown steeped-tea.

## And Then There Was a Disruption

Around the seventeenth or eighteenth century, farmers started to fertilize matcha. The tea's flavor probably became mellow and smooth from the combination of fertilizer and shading. Then in 1738, tea purveyor Soen Nagatani developed a new process called the "Uji method." First, harvested leaves were steamed. From there, if the leaves were dried and kneaded, the result was *gyokuro*, the only other shade-grown tea, though one that's steeped and sipped like fine brandy. If the leaves were steamed and not rolled out, they became *tencha*. The flat *tencha* leaves were then deveined, destemmed, ground, and *voila*: it's matcha. This process was more efficient than roasting and drying the tea leaves, and you know what efficiency means: matcha was brought to the people. Even today, this method is still standard throughout Japan.

## The Japanese Loosen Up

Before matcha could come to the United States, there needed to be a powdered green tea boom in modern-day Japan. The country first started exporting tea in 1610 through the Dutch East India Company out of Hirado, on the island of Kyushu. By the nineteenth century, 181 tons of it were being shipped overseas each year, including to the United States. But it was all steeped tea. That's because in Japan, matcha was rarefied. There were some regions where people drank matcha at home instead of steeped tea, but that was an exception to the rule. The mid- to late 1990s, however, saw a broader array of matcha products become popular in Japan (hello, green tea ice cream) due to producers starting to sell cheaper, culinary-grade powdered green

tea to be used in food as opposed to just the high-end, ceremonial grade stuff for drinking. Even Japanese Starbucks got in on the rise and began serving matcha au laits in the early aughts.

Around this time, matcha and its offshoots crept into the United States market through Japanese grocery stores in places with large Japanese communities, such as Los Angeles, San Francisco, and Hawaii. Simultaneously, Japanese culture became cool in America—think anime, manga, Gwen Stefani, even green tea lattes, which American Starbucks started offering around 2010.

## The Americanization of Matcha

As the United States transitioned from first wave coffee (Maxwell House, Folgers) to second wave (Starbucks), to third wave (Blue Bottle, Counter Culture, Stumptown), matcha was able to ride the tide. After all, coffee is about energy, as is matcha. But with coffee you crash; with matcha you don't—and it provides a sense of calm and mental clarity. Plus, with coffee, you don't get 100 percent of the health benefits from the bean; with matcha, you do.

Meanwhile, for years chai was the intermediate beverage for non-coffee drinkers who weren't necessarily tea fans. But the popularity of chai has leveled off. (Tea experts say the peak was when Oprah released her own chai brand in 2014.) So when the market started looking for the next beverage darling after third wave coffee, matcha fell in line as both a coffee alternative and an approachable tea that can be hot or cold, and sweet or savory.

Matcha occupies an interesting place between tea and coffee. It's a tea, with all of tea's wellness properties, but the weight and viscosity on the palate is closer to coffee. So matcha has the perfect blend of health benefits and flavor, kind of like how Kendall Jenner received just the right amount of Jenner and Kardashian.

## Other Influences and Influencers

But perhaps the biggest win for matcha in the United States has been, wait for it…Instagram. No joke: Most tea authorities actually attribute the drink's rise to social media. Matcha is the most photogenic of all tea products. When you have a sexy, stylish, yogic woman pictured with a green drink in her hand, and she looks about as cool as it gets, the drink must be about as cool as it gets.

The powdered green tea also has a nutritional profile and metabolic boost that gets headlines. Health gurus, such as Dr. Andrew Weil and Dr. Mehmet Oz, and celebs (yes, Ms. Goop again) love it. They've all built bridges to connect their audiences with a new go-to ingredient with zero drawbacks. Plus, matcha, which can naturally turn baked or cooked food an artificial-looking green, is more consistent with people's attitudes with farm-to-table eating. A chef doesn't want to add green dye #7 to his hand-churned butter, you know?

## Which Brings Us to Today

Whereas matcha was once esoteric, it's now popular and very much in demand. Matcha bar owners around the country say that when they started selling matcha—some up to twenty years ago—it always required an explanation. Now customers are coming in already obsessed. And you know something has hit the mainstream when food critics get ahold of it: In the *New York Times*, Florence Fabricant wrote about the matcha pie from Brooklyn's Four & Twenty Blackbirds, and in the *LA Times*, restaurant critic Jonathan Gold penned a piece on matcha chicken-liver mousse from Cannibal, in Culver City. The hope among matcha insiders is that the powder will become a staple in the American pantry, as soy sauce did when it entered the United States' cooking repertoire after World War II.

## What's Next?

The latest trend in matcha is expanding the powder beyond the kitchen. In March 2016, the American contemporary artist Tom Sachs debuted an exhibition at New York's The Noguchi Museum called "Tom Sachs: Tea Ceremony," in which he explored his take on the Way of Tea. (It involved a Ritz cracker, an Oreo wagashi, and a ceramic bowl embellished with the NASA logo.) The beauty world has caught on to the powdered stuff, using it in baths (mixing matcha, water, epsom salts, and essential oils) and face masks (blending matcha, Greek yogurt, honey, coconut oil, and aloe). We're even hearing rumors of a forthcoming matcha toothpaste.

Don't, however, expect to see the tea ceremony making an appearance in the United States any time soon. The ritual isn't like karate, which can be practiced with a bathrobe and a mirror. The Way of Tea will likely never become a big Japanese export, though purists do worry that matcha's Japanese context will be left behind as the tea becomes more accessible in the United States. Matcha is a delicate powder created by artisans, and an enormous amount of effort goes into each sip. Can Westerners appreciate that? The fear of losing authenticity is why tea connoisseurs advocate that people learn how to make matcha, not just drink it, and why matcha bar owners champion watching your matcharista whip up your drink. Doing so presents a moment for you to experience gratitude and quiet joy.

## Ten Things to Know About the Japanese Tea Ceremony

*Chanoyu*, the Japanese word for tea ceremony, literally means "hot water for tea." A traditional ritual can take up an entire afternoon, and you have better things to do with your time—that SoulCycle bike isn't going to set itself up. So here's the gist of it, based on our personal experience in Japan.

### 1. It's interactive art

While the tea ceremony is a cultural and esoteric experience, it is not a comfortable one. The emphasis on perfectionism creates tension. Think of it as participatory art rather than a tea party. You aren't there to relax or contribute witty rhetoric; you are there to watch, observe, and appreciate.

### 2. Stretch first

You will sit on your shins—*virasana* style in yoga—for a really long time. Your legs will start to hurt. They will fall asleep. And when you finally stand up, you will feel like a peg-legged pirate. It's okay to move your legs if sitting becomes unbearable, but it's sort of frowned upon. Then again, you will never see these people again in your life… and you will see your legs every day.

### 3. Lots of bowing

Your cotillion curtseying is no good here.

### 4. Misty Copeland you are not

No matter what you think, you aren't elegant. Especially when you have to slide across the floor in a manner that feels like using your arms like a monkey. You will mess up. A LOT. The host has rehearsed his or her performance for perhaps thirty years. Your first tea ceremony is like going to your first dance cardio class and having flashbacks to being the husky child ballerina in the back row.

### 5. No white socks, no service

You will need to wear them in order to walk on the tatami mat floor in the tea room. Speaking of tatami mats, no stepping on the cracks (it's a Japanese superstition).

### 6. No talking

SHHHHHHH! No, seriously.

### 7. Yet another no: no substitutions

The tea made in the ceremony is prepared the way it should be: using a whisk, water, and a bowl. Do not expect to get served a Westernized matcha with milk. And do not ask for a latte (see number 6).

### 8. Treats!

*Wagashi*, or Japanese sweets, are eaten before drinking matcha—on the host's cue, of course—to cut the tea's bitterness. These are not American confections like agave gummy bears or ZenBunni Shiva Rose chocolate. The "treats" are often made from rice and bean paste.

### 9. Admire the ceramics

Bowls are the traditional tea ceremony drinking vessel, and many Japanese collect them the way Justin Bieber collects obnoxious cars—that is, to the extreme. They aren't sets, but individual pieces. You will look at and admire your unique one. Look at the right side, the left side, the front, and the back. Then at the right and to the left again. (If you are Beyoncé, *to the left, to the left*.)

### 10. Slurp it up

The tea ceremony is one time when it is okay to slurp. In fact, slurping the last sip implies you are finished and satisfied.

### Bonus round: enjoy it

All this said, the tea ceremony is about community, gathering, and taking the time to host someone. That person-to-person experience is something that is lost in today's disconnected world. Love the moment for what it is. Snapchat can wait.

## Tea Ceremony Tools

### 1. Chawan
A bowl available in a wide range of sizes and styles

### 2. Natsume
The small lidded container or caddy in which the matcha is placed

### 3. Chashaku
A bamboo scoop used to measure tea from the caddy into the bowl

### 4. Chasen
A bamboo whisk used to mix the powdered tea with hot water

### 5. Hishaku
A long bamboo ladle used to transfer hot water from the pot into the bowl

### 6. Kama
An iron or copper pot used to heat up the water

## The Trendy Beverage Timeline

### 2500 BC – Matcha

Shennong, the father of Chinese medicine, is said to have gotten the Chinese hooked on the elixir five thousand years ago. The drink was then popularized throughout the world by three important people: tea saint Lu Yü in China in 760, Buddhist monk Myōan Eisai in Japan in 1191, and Gwyneth Paltrow in the United States in 2015, when she Instagrammed a picture of hers from the matcha bar Chalait in New York.

### 221 BC – Kombucha

The Chinese brewed this remedy from mushrooms eons ago. In the United States, hippies got into fermented black or green tea in the 1960s, and AIDS patients revived it in Los Angeles in the 1990s. Today, health-focused restaurants have it on tap.

### 1200s – Bulletproof Libations

In 2009, entrepreneur and biohacker Dave Asprey first blogged about Bulletproof Coffee, a blend of low mold coffee, grass-fed butter and medium-chain triglyceride oil. The drink hit the mainstream a few years later, around 2014. However, Asprey had adapted the beverage from yak butter tea, which has been a staple in Tibet since the thirteenth century.

### 1600s – Switchel

Water, vinegar, and ginger, often sweetened with molasses, honey, brown sugar, or maple syrup, became a summer hydration staple in the American colonies. Vermont hipsters brought the drink back to life circa 2013.

### 1700s – Bone Broth

In France long ago, innkeepers used to give travelers *restoratifs*, otherwise known as the liquid that remains after animal bones are boiled in water. Bone-broth shops started appearing in New York in 2014, and the trend spread throughout the country.

### 1940s – Juice Cleansing

Stanley Burroughs invented the lemon juice, maple syrup, and cayenne pepper fast in 1940 and reestablished it in 1976 in his book *The Master Cleanse*. The juice-as-food diet was resurrected in the early 2000s with the juice–based cleansing phenomenon that Hollywood became enamored with, and which...Gwyneth Paltrow made fashionable when she wrote about it on her website Goop in 2010.

### Ask the Expert:

*What was your vision behind your matcha bar, Cha Cha Matcha?*

As long as the people who are making matcha take it very seriously and are serving the highest-quality product at an affordable price, why can't everyone just have fun? We really felt that every tea and coffee shop had the same serious atmosphere, where you felt you needed to have knowledge of the drink. At our spot, we wanted fun music, fun people working in a relaxing environment. That was really important to us, and that's our take on matcha, too.

*Cha Cha is such a hot spot. Why do you think this is?*

There needs to be a culture behind matcha. It needs to be contemporary and young. And that's what we are trying to do with this place. Create a place you can go with your friends and be social, run into someone you know. And have a vibe and a face to it. People go and get a tin with Japanese writing on it and it doesn't really speak to them. We are trying to tell a story and speak to our customers and make them feel good and have fun when they drink tea.

**Matthew Morton**
*Cha Cha Matcha, New York City*

# Chapter 3
# The Matcha Lifestyle

## How to Find a Good Matcha Bar

Throughout the United States, matcha bar owners share a common goal of introducing matcha to a wider, curious audience; they are there to teach, not to judge. (Unless, that is, you are sporting a man bun and prominently displaying the latest installment of Karl Ove Knausgård's *My Struggle* so people know that you, too, long to make art in this creative void of a world. In that case, you deserve it.)

Your first matcha shot can be intense, perhaps a little confusing. *Is it bitter or sweet? Am I feeling energized or calm? Why are my lips stained green?* Then there is the intimidation of ordering. *Do I just order matcha or is there a special handshake? Should I ask for a specific grade? Can I add sweetener? Will the matcharista like me?*

The number of (legitimate) specialty matcha bars, while steadily increasing, is still limited. To help ease the insecurities of customers, very few places actually serve matcha the traditional way—you won't have the option of thick or thin, let alone have your tea served in a bowl. But you still want to find a place that offers high-quality matcha and prepares it well.

## The Matcharista

Matcharistas are the new baristas, but more healthy and less critical—even when you order three almond-milk matcha lattes for your "coworkers." The best ones go through extensive training, learning the history, health benefits, grades, and different ways to build matcha drinks. They can be a wealth of knowledge, and ultimately they want to educate so more people are comfortable experiencing matcha. Keep in mind that you aren't alone with your confusion. The most commonly asked questions in a matcha bar are:

*1. What is matcha?*
*2. What is your most popular drink?*
*3. Can I get it iced?*

Some customers just bring in a photo from Instagram, point, and say, "I want this." Matcharistas have seen and been asked it all. For example, one woman read online that the magnesium levels in Japan were making matcha toxic (not true), and another man wanted to know if matcha would cure his psoriasis (it won't).

Get to know your matcharista. Become a regular. You may get some sample tastings of new drinks or a free matcha hot chocolate after a disastrous Tinder date (like the one when the guy made his date retroactively pay him for the lattes and avocado toast...yikes). And yes, the matcharistas will happily spend time making sure your matcha latte art is perfect for #nofilter.

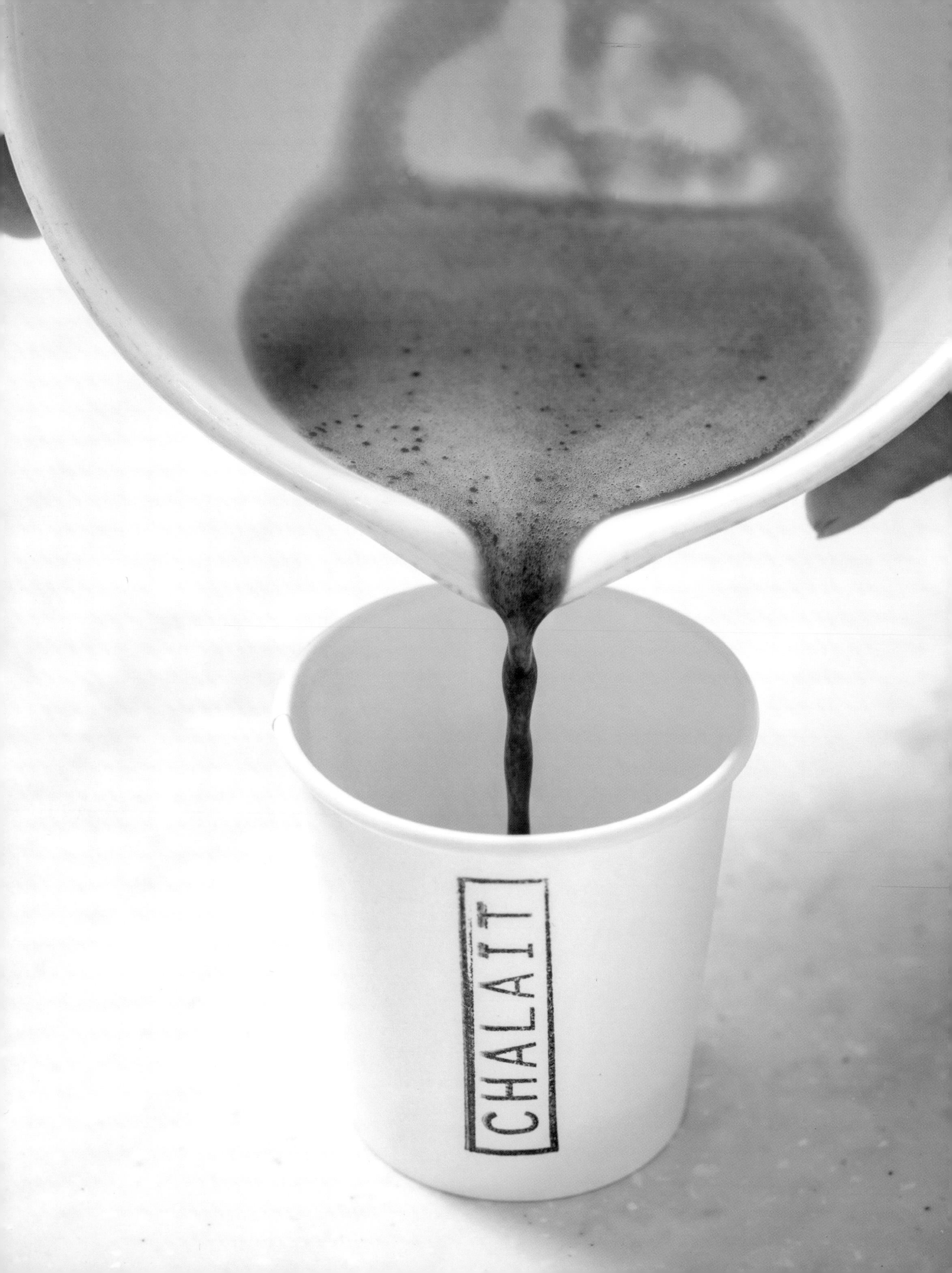
CHALAIT

## Ordering Matcha

Tell your matcharista exactly what you like and let him or her build a drink that you will personally enjoy. Matcha bars purposely offer espresso-style menus to help customers feel at ease. Staying with what you know will make the transition easier: Cortado or latte? Iced or hot? Sweetened or unsweetened? Whole milk or almond milk?

In lattes, most milks (whole, skim, almond, coconut, soy, macadamia, or hemp, you name it) will work fine. Coconut milk is often requested, but there's difficulty finding one that holds up to the matcha. Whole milk makes the prettiest latte art (see "The Froth on Top," page 41).

Though matcha is not traditionally sweetened, you're welcome to add sugar, honey, maple syrup, agave, stevia, or coconut sugar to your beverage. It's not illegal, nor is it frowned upon.

If you are unsure or don't have time to listen to a matcharista's initiatory spiel, the classic introductory drink is a matcha latte. The next step up is a matcha Americano (a matcha shot with a good amount of hot water) and a little sweetener. In the Americano, you can really taste the matcha, and the sweetener will mask some of the bitterness until you are more familiar with the taste. Once you are comfortable with matcha, try a ceremonial shot.

If you order a shot (or another short drink), sip it in the establishment, just like an espresso shot, though most places are happy to give it to you in a mini to-go cup. It's okay to get a double shot—and if you're living in the modern world, you probably need one.

One rising trend most matcharistas aren't fans of is customers wanting to add espresso to their matcha drinks. This cross-beverage breed is referred to as a "dirty matcha." In Italy, this request could be well-executed, because the Italian-style espresso base tends to be darker and fruitier, counterbalancing the matcha. But in the United States, the espresso base often skews to the bitter side, and when mixed with matcha it results in a drink that's exponentially bitter. If you really need a jolt, get a double matcha shot or a matcha drink with an espresso on the side.

## Matcha Bar Etiquette

There isn't as much snobbery in the matcha world as in the coffee world (at least not yet). But before you order, remember that every drink on the menu has its purpose and is served a specific way, with a specific amount of matcha, to bring out different flavor profiles. If you can think of it, the matcharistas have already tried it—and there is a reason why your idea isn't on the menu. Your order isn't an opportunity for you to do *you*.

Matcha bars usually make matcha drinks in smaller serving sizes to get the right ratio of matcha to liquid, so don't ask for a bigger cup. For example, if you have 2 grams of matcha and request 16 ounces of milk, you aren't going to taste the matcha. So ordering more milk or less ice isn't going to help you game the system and get more bang for your buck—it will just dilute the matcha flavor. Matcha bars aren't trying to rip you off. We promise!

Unlike specialty coffee shops filled with mustaches and plaid shirts hiding behind glaring laptop screens writing the next *Fight Club*, matcha bars tend to be more social (like IRL social). Friends meet up on weekends to hear about the latest relationship woes or to discuss the pros and cons of certain boutique fitness class instructors. We think they are called "bars"—and not "shops"—for a reason.

### Questions to Ask Matcharistas to Test Their Legitimacy

*1. What is matcha?*
Even you should know the right answer to this by now.

*2. Where do you source your matcha from?*
And this one, too.

*3. What grade do you use?*
A good response should be ceremonial, with bonus points if they say they use a finer grind for iced drinks.

*4. Can I see your matcha?*
You're checking the matcha powder for its bright-green color (brown or yellow-tinged powder = bad).

*5. How much matcha do you use?*
A good rule of thumb is 2 grams, or about 1 teaspoon, per drink. If they use less, ask them why they've picked this amount as a serving size.

*6. Do you use condensed milk in your matcha?*
There's nothing wrong with this other than it can be a sneaky way for a matcha bar to make your beverage sweeter.

## You May Have Found a Good Matcha Spot If...

• It stocks matcha from Japan—Uji specifically—and only serves ceremonial grade.

• A bamboo whisk is used to blend the matcha with hot water first, no matter the drink order. Extra points if the matcha is sifted and if the whisking is done in a bowl.

• The counter is constructed so you can watch your drink being prepared. This not only educates you, but it forces you to slow down and watch the process (aka getting your Zen on).

• At least half of the customers are Instagramming their vibrant-green lattes and using one or more of the following hashtags: #matcha#butfirstmatcha#matchaverymuch#itsprettyeasybeinggreen.

• Unsweetened or minimally sweetened nondairy milk options are stocked. If the matcha bar offers homemade almond or cashew milk, never leave.

• Vegan- and gluten-free pastries are on the menu, along with at least one food that respectfully uses matcha as an ingredient, such as a delish matcha parfait.

• Albums by David Bowie or Fleetwood Mac are on the speakers. Think retro cool.

• The color scheme is Japanese-style minimalist or Beverly Hills Hotel on acid. Remember, matcha is a tea of contradictions.

• At least one Tinder or Bumble date happens around you. If there is, grab a seat and watch the magic (or disaster). If you're the one on it, see "Impress Your Tinder or Bumble Date" (page 38).

• All customers aren't on their MacBooks creating a business plan for their app. A good matcha bar tends to be more social, with more conversations than typing (as we are sitting in one...typing).

• Gwyneth Paltrow is in front of you in line.

## Keep Walking If...

• The "matcha" is sourced from anywhere other than Japan. If the matcharistas say it's from a single-origin farm in Ethiopia, they are liars. Either way, leave.

• The matcha is anything but bright green.

• The matcharistas don't whisk or blend the matcha before building your drink, which is a one-way ticket to Clump City!

• The matcharistas use a minibaking whisk that looks like it was made for an American Girl® doll. Even Molly wouldn't have stooped so low. Maybe Felicity.

• The menu features a "green tea latte." By now you should know that not all green tea is created equal.

• The matcha comes artificially presweetened, in concentrate form, or mixed with powdered milk.

• The menu offers a 24-ounce latte. Are they also going to let you bathe in it?

• The food menu throws matcha in anything and everything. "I'll have a matcha latte, a matcha donut, and a matcha steak, please."

• There are too many man buns in your vicinity. Even one man bun is too many.

## An Ordering Cheat Sheet

*Ceremonial shot:*
Made with 2 grams of high-grade matcha blended or whisked with 2 ounces of hot water. This is the "shot" building block in all matcha drinks.

*Americano:*
A matcha shot with 8 to 12 ounces of hot water. Too much water will dilute the flavor, so always feel free to ask for less.

*Latte:*
*Latte* means "milk" in Italian, so you can deduce that you will get (steamed) milk with your matcha shot. Most places serve it with 12 ounces.

*Iced latte:*
Same as above, but served over ice. Matcha can be pretty and smart and cool and refreshing. You would have hated her in high school.

*Macchiato:*
A ceremonial shot mixed with a little bit of steamed milk. It's adorable.

*Cortado:*
A matcha shot with less milk than a latte but more milk than a macchiato. It's basically a skinny latte.

*Cappuccino:*
One part matcha shot, one part steamed milk, one part foam. A matcha trifecta.

*Iced tea:*
A matcha Americano served over ice.

*DEFCON:*
10 (ten!) grams of matcha with just enough hot water to make it potable. Taken down in one swig.

*Dirty matcha:*
Any matcha drink (usually an Americano or latte) with a shot of espresso in it. It might not taste good, but it might help you conquer the world.

## Impress Your Tinder or Bumble Date

Matcha-tasting notes aren't as particular as in, say, the wine world, so have fun with them. Say you can really taste the "raw cacao and butterscotch," "earthy green vegetables," or "sweet potato drizzled with butter." Compliment your date by saying the matcha is "balanced and complex," or "easy and awesome," just like her (or him).

• If you are at restaurant or bar that offers matcha, ask the bartender to make you a matcha cocktail. You're cultured. No big deal.

• Order a ceremonial shot. Matcha is kind of your thing.

• Tell your date you're a regular. But only do this if you *are* a regular, so it's not weird to high-five the matcharista.

• Tell your date you own the matcha bar. But do this only if you're Matthew Morton (see page 29).

• Tell your date that ceremonial-grade matcha uses only the top two leaves of the tea plant, so drinking it is like playing a game of "just the tips."

## Dealing with Matcha Lip and Teeth Stain

Your matcha drink may leave you looking like you just made out with an alien, and we don't mean Alf (Freudian field day here). With matcha lip and teeth stain, the struggle is real. It's most noticeable from drinking hot milk-based matcha drinks, and the stain sticks more readily to lipglossed lips. But it's easily dealt with. A makeup- or lipstick-removing cloth is most efficient. A napkin works, but the paper may stick to your lips. When in doubt, just use the back of your hand. Our matcharista friends assure us that it's perfectly acceptable to tell someone they have the stain. They do it all the time. So if your matcharista makes eye contact and points to his lips, he isn't trying to be fresh; he's helping you conquer the day without a green smile.

## Faster, Stronger, Better

In Silicon Valley, start-up junkies down a so-called DEFCON level of matcha, which is 10 grams per shot (as a refresher, 2 grams is a regular portion). A mini-DEFCON is 5 grams. Both make for one very thick cup of matcha. The DEFCON addicts don't care about the flavor. They have zero interest in that. All they want is the tea's psychoproductive effects. They just put 10 grams in a cup of water, shake it, force it down, and become superhuman. Eric Gower, founder of San Francisco's Breakaway Matcha, which sources, custom blends, and distributes powdered green tea, has created matcha programs at Twitter, Airbnb, Square, Evernote, and Zynga for this reason: people at these companies are essentially using it as a productivity tool. It's a healthy step down from Modafinil.

## The Instagramability of Matcha

The aesthetics of matcha have made it an Instagram darling. It reflects the perfect social media persona: healthy, trendy, pretty, and cultish. Posting a photo of matcha is an incredibly simple way to complexly define oneself, to say, "I care, but I don't care" in latte form. Matcharistas tell us that about three in four customers snap a photo of their matcha with their phones. We've been told some customers will actually order both a coffee and a matcha, take a picture of the matcha, throw it away, and leave with their coffee. This hurts our hearts. We may start a rescue organization for discarded matchas. Throwing

away $6 a day on a matcha latte for a social media persona? Can you write it off on your taxes as a business expense?

Do ask your matcharista for a specific latte art design that fits your posting mood. Since most intricate designs are done with stencils, don't request something impossible. Stick with a basic free-pour design (see "The Froth on Top," page 41). Some matcharistas may be up for a challenge—one of ours nailed a swan!—but don't be offended if they're not. It's harder than it looks. Want to be different? One of the most aesthetically pleasing drinks is a matcha hot chocolate. If made right, the rich brown and creamy green swirl perfectly together, and the cocoa sprinkles add a magical dusting—#suckitothermatchaphotos.

## #Matcha Hashtag Ideas

*#loveyousomatcha  #itsprettyeasybeinggreen
#hitmewithyourbestshot  #matchamatchaman
#matchamemucho  #leangreendrinkingmachine
#momatchanoproblems  #makematchanotwar
#whiskitgood  #letitfroth  #matchamadeinheaven*

# Confessions from Anonymous Matcharistas

Like everyone in the service industry, matcharistas know their stuff, and sometimes they know everybody else's stuff as well (they try not to listen, but come on, sometimes people are asking for it). Regardless of whether you are a curious first timer or a serious *koicha* connoisseur, there's always a gem of wisdom to be had from those on the front lines of matcha mayhem.

### What is the most popular drink that you serve?

**Matcharista #1:** Matcha latte with almond milk. Hot or iced depending on the season.

**Matcharista #2:** Coconut milk matcha lattes, hot or iced.

### What latte art do you like to make?

**Matcharista #1:** I'm old school. I always do a tulip or heart.

**Matcharista #2:** Ten hearts. I want to compete in a latte art competition. It took me three months to become good at it.

### Do you sell more coffee or matcha?

**Matcharista #3:** When we first opened, in 2014, we were getting about 75 to 80 percent coffee to matcha. Now we have coffee favored 60 to 40 percent in the morning, and then matcha 60 to 40 percent in the evening.

### What kind of person comes into your shop?

**Matcharista #1:** Lots of young professionals. Yogis. Folks who live a really healthy lifestyle. Lots of people from SoulCycle and Equinox. During Fashion Week, models and designers.

**Matcharista #2:** Millennials. Hipsters.

### Who's been your most unique customer?

**Matcharista #1:** A drunk guy dressed as a banana. And there was a dominatrix with a gimp who had a ball in his mouth. By the end of the order he was kissing the dominatrix's feet. And he still had to pay for the matcha.

### What are your busiest times?

**Matcharista #1:** The weekends, once that brunch hour hits. Mornings are definitely busy. We get a second wave in the afternoon.

**Matcharista #2:** The weekends. We always have lines out the door.

### Any secret drinks not on the menu?

**Matcharista #1:** The most recent addition is The Shrub. It's basically fresh fruit, citrus, sugar, and apple cider vinegar. It has that vinegary taste but is really refreshing. If you add the matcha to the shrub, it surprisingly combines really well.

### What are some ordering tips?

**Matcharista #3:** A lot of people will walk in and say, "Just give me the best matcha." And it's not about what my favorite is. We'll ask: Do you drink coffee? Do you like your coffee straight up? Do you like a latte in the morning? And do you like your latte sweetened or unsweetened? You work with them to match what they usually like as a starting point.

### What's the worst matcha drink someone has ordered?

**Matcharista #3:** One request that is happening more frequently than we would like is matcha and coffee. Which never works. It's basically a naturally bitter component with another naturally bitter component. I think people are just more curious than anything. They just want to know what it's like. It's not going to be good.

### How much matcha is in your drinks?

**Matcharista #1:** We do 2 grams, or 1 teaspoon, of matcha per drink, which is a healthy serving of matcha.

**Matcharista #2:** Same. That's the standard. It's a real problem when other matcha bars use less, because it rips off the customer and undercuts the market.

### What's the most number of shots that someone has ordered?

**Matcharista #1:** Three drinks, all with extra shots of matcha. One of them is a latte and the other is a matcha iced tea. And the other one—a latte or an iced tea—is depending on her mood. She does this every morning. That's nine shots of matcha per day.

### Are there a lot of Tinder dates at your matcha bar?

**Matcharista #1:** Way more than I expected. My general rule of thumb is I don't get involved. Because it's drama.

**Matcharista #3:** There have been some great ones where you know they wish we had alcohol on the menu. There are definitely some people who love making out in public.

## The Froth on Top

While matcharistas can make green-with-Instagram-envy hearts, rosettes, and tulips appear out of nowhere in white milk foam, matcha latte art is much more difficult than it looks. And it's impossible to create at home, unless you own a $16,000 La Marzocco espresso machine. If you do, please be our friend.

Design work requires mastering another art form first: milk steaming. And without the proper equipment, well…good luck. A commercial steaming wand is a must. Why? Because milk is made of fat, sugar, and proteins, and when it is injected with high-pressure air—preferably 1 to 1.5 bars of it—and rapidly heated to 130° to 140° Fahrenheit, the proteins unravel. This breaks down the fat and sugar. Scientists call this *denaturing*; matcharistas call it creating the microfoam and

velvety smooth texture needed for latte art. You can't create microfoam with anything else. The fact that this process also makes milk taste sweeter is a bonus.

Whole milk is best for designs because its fat bonds the milk and foam. One or 2 percent milk is also okay, but nonfat skim is trickier. Almond or soy milk are also hard, but either one works if the milk has a binding agent, such as xanthan gum.

The matcha itself should be on the thicker side to get good color contrast. Watch as the matcharista holds the pitcher of steamed milk 6 inches above the matcha cup, which is tilted at a 45° angle, and then pours the milk into the center of the matcha in a swirling motion. When the cup is two-thirds full, the matcharista lowers the pitcher so it almost touches the tea. The milk starts to appear in the middle like a white cloud—this is the base—and then the matcharista pulls the pitcher back up so only a trickle of milk is pulled through the base (to make a heart or tulip) or zigzagged before being pulled through (for the rosette). These are the three main free-pouring designs. The fancy art on social media is done with etching tools.

Need help to remember this sequence? Try this secret latte-art rhyme that matcharistas use:

*High and slow,*
*Then go down low,*
*Increase the flow,*
*And there you go.*

Getting the hang of latte art, we're told, takes three to six months—assuming there's an unlimited supply of milk and matcha to practice with. Our barista at Toby's Estate in New York City, which offers latte art classes, says he's yet to have a customer order a specific type of latte art. He also assures us that he doesn't do better designs for nicer customers. All art is created equal.

# Chapter 4
# Matcha at Home

## Buying Matcha

Quality matcha engages all foodie senses: color, smell, flavor, texture, and finish. Cracking a tin of it is kind of like opening a fresh can of tennis balls—*pssst, vrack, sniff, ahhhh*! If good matcha were a celebrity, it would be Gwen Stefani, circa 2005, during her Harajuku-girl phase. If bad matcha were famous, it would be Tara Reid, circa 2014, post-plastic surgery with an ample supply of Juicy Couture velour jumpsuits. Here's what to consider in order to make sure you purchase the former.

### Source

The country of origin should be noted on the tin. Look for Japan. Always. The specific Japanese region won't necessarily be listed, but if you can find Uji, Nishio, or Fukuoka mentioned anywhere, all the better.

Let's discuss Uji for a minute. The reason this region grows such good matcha has to do with its *terroir*, that combination of factors—including climate, soil, and sunlight—that gives certain crops their distinct character. Uji is in a valley, which contributes to its matcha's uniqueness. The valley is slightly below sea level and extremely humid. We mean extreme. It's unbearable in June and July, and very, very wet. There's a rainy season that compounds the humidity. Farmers happily grow matcha here, where they baby their plants in an obsessive manner. But the Japanese, in general, also place a lot of cultural weight on Uji. It's the old tea capital, and a lot of the tea ceremony schools have been buying matcha from the area for a very long time. And people

are loyal in Japan. Once they find a source they like, they tend to keep returning to it forever. The emperor, for example, and the entire imperial family, has always sourced its matcha from various places in Uji. This acts as social proof of the region's quality: if the emperor is getting his tea from Uji, then all the other fancy people who drink matcha also get it from there.

The thing to keep in mind about Uji is that it produces a very small amount of matcha. Even though it sounds like a matcha Mecca, and it is, the number of farms involved is small. The rest of it is produced by large corporations in areas such as Nishio, which produce bigger quantities at lower costs.

Why should you avoid buying matcha from somewhere other than Japan? There are reports that some countries will grind up any green tea leaf and call it "matcha." There are also concerns about toxic soil in some regions. Matcha experts are quick to note that while they approve of and are loyal to Japanese matcha, they are not saying that great matcha can't be grown in other places with optimal tea-growing conditions, rather they are saying that at the moment, no one other than you-know-who has perfected matcha.

### Color

Matcha should be vibrant green: think hallucinogenic, acid rock, and anime. It should scream "Look at me!"—but it's too modest to do

that. Matcha shouldn't look like camouflage. Dark-green and yellow hues mean it's bad matcha, from older tea leaves or ones that have been heated during processing. Because matcha usually comes in a tin or sealed bag, it's hard to identify the color when purchasing. But if you open the matcha and it doesn't look right, don't be shy about returning it.

## Grade

There are two grades of matcha: ceremonial (for drinking with water and very small amounts of milk) and culinary (for anything else). There are also subgrades within both grades; the most common is "everyday grade," which falls somewhere between ceremonial and culinary. Ceremonial grade uses the tea plant's top two leaves—the newest, baby buds—whereas culinary grade uses rougher leaves lower down on the plant. Ceremonial is also usually ground old-school style with a slowly turning granite mill, which makes a more granular powder, as small as 5 microns. To put it into perspective, it takes more than one hour to pulverize 30 grams of matcha by stone. There aren't many people in the world who have the legacy knowledge to perform granite grinding. For mass production, large ceramic balls quickly do the work, which can heat up the leaves and turn them brown and bitter.

Since ceremonial grade matcha is traditionally mixed with just hot water, it has a sweeter, smoother, more pronounced flavor, and it leaves a silky finish in your mouth. Culinary-grade matcha is more bitter, which is fine because the astringency dissipates when the tea is combined with other ingredients. This is why it's okay to use culinary grade in larger milk-based drinks. Older leaves and more conventional grinding methods do make culinary-grade tea less expensive to produce, and therefore less expensive to buy.

Some matcha distributors sell matcha specifically used for iced matcha drinks. This matcha has a very fine grind.

## Price

It's easy to get wrapped up in the cost of matcha: people can get pretty freaked out about it. Twenty dollars for 30 grams seems expensive. But one serving (two grams) shakes out to be about $2. So for just $2 a day, you can have a world-class drink that will provide you with focus and an in-the-zone quality, and it's full of antioxidants. Do expect to pay $20 to $35 (or more) for 30 grams of ceremonial grade.

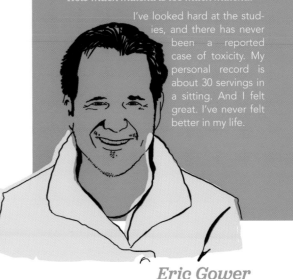

## Ask the Expert:

*What's one unique attribute of a high-end matcha?*

Quality matchas have these really long finishes—you swallow it and it's still on your palette for a good thirty seconds to one minute, sometimes two minutes. It should still have that kind of singing taste.

*What's the most expensive matcha in the world?*

The most expensive one I've seen is 50,000 yen, which is roughly $500 for 30 grams, or $33 per serving. Where it gets really wacky and expensive is when you get to the bowls and tools. I saw a bowl for $250,000. The Japanese are pretty comfortable paying high prices for ceramics. Most Japanese families don't mind shelling out for ones that give them pleasure, and that's something that Americans have not understood and just don't do.

*How has the matcha boom changed the lives of the farmers?*

These guys are the salt of the earth and they work so hard, and it's great that there has been a boost in demand for them. Their lifestyles are different. One of the guys I've been dealing with for a long time picked me up in a lovely BMW.

*How much matcha is too much matcha?*

I've looked hard at the studies, and there has never been a reported case of toxicity. My personal record is about 30 servings in a sitting. And I felt great. I've never felt better in my life.

*Eric Gower*
*Breakaway Matcha, San Anselmo, California*

Anything cheaper than this and you aren't getting a deal—you are getting bad matcha. Culinary matcha tends to be slightly less expensive, hovering around $15 for 30 grams; again, it's fine to buy this grade if you drink matcha with larger amounts of milk or cook with it.

## Organic?

Ah, the magic O word. With the rise of health-conscious and eco-friendly consumers, an organic label is often preferred. But the world's finest matchas, without a doubt, are inorganic—no ifs, ands, or buts. This is because matcha is what one might call a "tortured plant." Since it spends its last few weeks in the shade, it doesn't get the energy it needs from the sun for photosynthesis. When plants don't get light, they die. For plants to stay alive, they need large quantities of nitrogen, which often comes from inorganic fertilizer. The other issue is that matcha is a monocrop. The farmers grow beautiful single bushes, which attract parasites and insects that are hard to manage without some form of pesticide.

Organic matcha tends to be a little limp, dead, and nonvibrant. Uji farmers aren't really into it, complaining that it doesn't taste good, and they are usually right. And you have to remember that a lot of people growing matcha are in their seventies, eighties, and nineties, and they don't want to be told what to do. They also aren't awake to the fact that there is a huge world marketplace for organic matcha. Plus, transitioning to organic matcha requires a complete replanting or expansion into new farmland, which means it can take up to five years for the first organic harvest, making it a costly endeavor.

There are younger, more globally aware farmers in southern Japan, where the weather is subtropical. These farmers are making great

| A Buying Guide | Good Matcha | Bad Match |
|---|---|---|
| Color | Vibrant green | Army green or yellow |
| Price | $20 to $35+ (per 30 grams) | Usually less than $20 (per 30 grams) |
| Taste | Sweet and umami | Bitter and astringent |
| Texture | Finely ground, smooth, and silky | Coarse and rough |
| Reminds us of | Gwen Stefani in 2005 | Tara Reid in 2014 |

progress with the organic stuff, and it is more readily available now than ten years ago. For now, however, organic matcha is almost always lower in quality in terms of flavor, nutrients, and color.

## Blends

Tea experts combine different matcha grades to create blends. There is no quality or price differentiation for single-plant matcha versus a blend.. Blends are given poetic names and handed down through tea-master lineages, but the number of blends is limited, and the same blend—even one in just a different size tin—may have a different name given to it by a different tea master. Think of it like this: J.Crew changes the names of its colors every season, but is there really a difference between salmon or coral when it comes to cashmere? (Chinos, maybe.) Similarly, the blend names are more a means of marketing than an actual differentiator of quality.

## Texture

Look for finely ground powder. Or smooth and silky, like creamy eye shadow. If the powder is rough and grainy, like sand, it hasn't been ground properly and will leave clumps in your tea.

## Shelf Life

The "best by" date is a big indicator that the producer or seller is serious about making sure you are getting good tea. If there is no expiration date, the seller has consciously chosen to not include one, which reflects the brand's commitment (or lack of) to quality.

## Storing Matcha

Matcha is sensitive to light, heat, and humidity. It oxidizes quickly, so proper care is imperative. High-quality matcha comes in a tin that blocks light. For home storage, you should avoid clear glass containers for this reason. A vacuum-seal lid that pushes air out will help keep moisture at bay.

Proper storage will extend the shelf life and ensure that the bright-green color, umami taste, and silky texture are preserved in every scoop. Unlike wine, older isn't better with matcha. Unopened matcha lasts approximately one year, and it should be enjoyed within a month after opening to get the most expressive flavor.

Refrigeration is a point of debate; some say it preserves freshness, others claim it can introduce too much moisture to the fickle powder, and still others say to refrigerate unopened matcha but to store it at room temperature once opened. But once you get hooked on matcha, it probably won't be around long enough for you to worry about keeping it fresh. A good rule of thumb is to buy small amounts and move through it quickly.

## Matcha's Dirty Little Secret

There is no regulation surrounding the use of the word *matcha*. The Japanese don't have a standard for it, and neither does the U.S. Department of Agriculture. Many matcha sellers outside of Japan lack integrity. Anyone can call literally anything matcha (which makes a great dog name, BTW). Another thing that's not regulated? The word *ceremonial*. Ceremonial tea is not something that has to taste or be processed a certain way, so you might be paying extra for a made-up label. Theoretically, a distributor could buy ground-up green tea sencha for $9 per pound from some unscrupulous guy on the Internet, make a really nice marketing plan and labels, and sell "ceremonial matcha" for $30 a tin. It's very difficult to know what is what when it comes to matcha, and nobody is monitoring the situation.

The consumer—you and us—is the one to feel sorry for. There you are standing in your health-food store or perusing Amazon. You've heard matcha is good for you. You've seen it on your Instagram feed. And now you have it in front of you. You can't open the can and look at its contents, which is the main way to know whether what you're buying is legit or not. The color is going to be a dead giveaway of quality, unless there is something really freaky going on, like a manufacturer adding some kind of neon-green dye to embellish the quality of its tea. Your only choice is to trust the label, which is a risky gambit.

Another problem with the lack of matcha regulation is that matcha bars can take shortcuts, such as sourcing tea from somewhere other than Japan and calling it "matcha," or just dumping green tea powder into a cup of almond milk with ice and calling it an "iced matcha latte." And if the matcha isn't made right, the consumer's first experience could be "I don't like this," or "it's bitter," and he'll never order it again. That's unfortunate, because a lot of times a poor matcha experience is all about how it was prepared.

For these reasons, we advocate cultivating a relationship with a trusted matcha seller or matcha bar (see "Resources," page 170).

It would take quite an effort on the part of the Japanese government to impose a set of matcha rules in the same way that Champagne producers did in their effort to prevent cava and other sparkling wines from being called Champagne. Wine producers, for example, are very organized. They benefit from laws and regulations. It's not the same with tea. One day there may be an effort to create and enforce rules on behalf of matcha producers, but for now the Japanese government really hasn't paid attention to the possibility of disingenuous marketing that could happen with the matcha boom. Quality matcha distributors and matcha bars throughout the United States are doing their best to create materials and standards that market matcha in a clear way, but all this stuff takes time to unfold.

## Some Like It Hot

Water temperature affects the taste of matcha. The water should never be boiling: 176° Fahrenheit is ideal. If it's hotter than that, the water can cook the powder, causing a bitter taste. If you don't have a kettle that measures temperature, bring the water to a boil, then transfer the water to a cup, then pour that cup of water into the vessel with matcha in it. This double transfer is the perfect amount of time for the water to drop to the right temperature.

## Drinking Bowls

Some matcha traditionalists believe the shape of the drinking bowl, like that of a wine glass, can affect the tasting experience. They argue that the size determines how the tea lands on the appropriate taste receptors in the mouth. In the winter they use taller bowls to keep the tea warmer, and in the summer they use wider ones to allow the tea to cool quicker. Other matcha experts say the bowl is just more formal—that it doesn't make the matcha taste better but rather is about tradition. Regardless, you can still enjoy matcha in the free coffee mug you got for switching insurance companies. We won't tell.

## Caring for Your Chasen

There are more than 120 kinds of Japanese bamboo *chasen*, or tea whisks, and the majority of them are hand-made by thirty or so craftsmen who are mostly located in Nara, Japan, about 25 miles south of Kyoto. The fewer and harder the bristles a whisk has, the stronger and more bitter the matcha will taste. The more and softer the bristles, the frothier the matcha will be. Do not put your whisk in the dishwasher or use detergent to clean it. Rinse it under running water, and use your fingers to wipe off the matcha. To avoid mold, let it dry completely on a whisk stand before storing.

## Traveling with Matcha

Although matcha is breaking through the beverage clutter we find at bars, restaurants, and grocers, it isn't easy finding places that serve it when we travel—or more importantly, serve it right. Luckily, matcha is an easy luxury to bring with you, keeping your daily ritual intact. Matcha tins are small, and unlike coffee beans, matcha doesn't cause your suitcase to smell like a Costa Rican coffee farm. Many brands are starting to make single-serve packages. They are easily transportable and especially great for trips that require minimal packing or weight, whether it's an overnight camping trip to Joshua Tree or climbing Mount Kilimanjaro.

Sometimes we order steamed milk from a coffee bar to add to our matcha to make a latte—some nice baristas even mix it for us (thank you, Blue Bottle!). If you are a purist, you can travel with your bamboo whisk and store it in a special whisk caddy to avoid damage, but a great alternative is a battery-powered milk frother. It's slender and efficient, but you might get some questionable looks if it accidentally goes off in your carry-on. We've used milk frothers on planes and in restaurants. People may throw tea shade your way while they drink their crappy free hotel coffee. You'll be too calm and focused to care.

## The Mindfulness of Matcha

Matcha is rooted in a ceremony that causes one to slow down, to treasure the moment. Translating that into today's culture can be virtually impossible. While the tea ceremony itself will most likely never become popular in the West, the modern preparation of matcha brings with it a new ritual, a way to spend just two minutes appreciating the act of chilling out and making a cup of tea.

Matcha is a labor of love. Farmers in Japan handpick each and every leaf from the tea plant, personally deveining and destemming each one before manually grinding them into the delicate powder. The tins on the shelf are usually bagged by a person, not a machine. By drinking the tea, you are appreciating the careful work of these farmers and their deep lineage. Whether at home or at a matcha bar, observing the matcha process invites you to stop and smell the roses—the mellow, floral, honeydew roses that linger on your tongue and bring a sense of calm. Like life, matcha is bittersweet. And without the bitterness of life, you wouldn't be able to enjoy the sweetness.

## A Matcha Meditation

*By Chloe Kernaghan and Krissy Jones, cofounders of Sky Ting Yoga in New York City*

In our view, meditation can happen in many forms, whether you're in an upright seat, a restorative pose, or in a state of conscious awareness where you allow yourself to be absorbed into the work you're doing. A morning ritual has become vital for our daily activities, helping to start the day off on the right foot, with a clear and calm purpose.

Preparing matcha can be a perfect opportunity to drop into this focus. In older lineages, when preparing an offering to be placed on an altar, one makes the food while chanting a mantra, allowing the mind to be entirely absorbed in the task and endowing the food with the love and care. We believe in the saying "you are what you eat," so why not take a moment to appreciate the process of making tea? If you have a personal mantra, you can add it into the mix; otherwise, have a single focus with each part of the tea experience:

• Seep in the bright-green color of the powder, paying attention to your measure as you scoop it into your bowl.

• Notice the ripple effects of the water as it hits the powder.

• As you begin to whisk, follow the movement of the tea as it suspends, seeing if all other thoughts in your mind might suspend—even for just a moment—right alongside it.

• Relish the froth, perhaps even eliciting a smile.

• When the tea is ready to drink, take a seat, and without doing anything else—no conversations, no emails, no TV on in the background—allow yourself to enjoy what you've created.

• Close your eyes and savor the texture, the flavors on the palate, the warmth of the tea.

## How to Make a Hot Matcha Drink

You're going to need matcha (obviously), liquid, something to whisk or blend the tea with, and something to serve it in. While tea ceremony tools are not necessary for making Americanized matcha, they do play cultural and practical roles. Plus, they look pretty awesome in your kitchen.

| | *Traditional Japanese Water-Based Method, Served in a Bowl* | *Modern American Latte Method, Served in a Cup* |
|---|---|---|
| *Scoop* | For thin matcha, use a *chashaku*, or bamboo tea scoop, to measure 1 scoop of powder. For thick matcha, use 3 scoops. | Measure about 2 grams, or 1 teaspoon, of powder. |
| *Sift* | Hold a fine-mesh sieve over a bowl. Sift the matcha to break up clumps, which are caused by static electricity. Use the tip of the *chasen*, or bamboo whisk, to break up any remaining clumps that made their way into the bowl. | Use a stainless steel sieve over a cup. |
| *Pour* | For thin matcha, add about ¼ cup (2 ounces) of almost boiling water—176°F to be exact—to the powder that has been sieved into the bowl. You can always add more water if it's too thick, but once it's too thin, you can't really add more matcha; you have to start all over. For thick matcha, pour slightly less water into the bowl. | Ditto. |
| *Blend* | For thin matcha, whisking in a W formation across the bowl is most common; this creates an espresso-like crema. Whatever you do, never use an M formation. (Yes, that's a joke.) For thick matcha, massage the powder using an N to create a consistency more like warm honey. | To blend the matcha, use a cocktail or protein shaker, a milk frother, or a blender. A spoon will not get the job done. After mixing the matcha, add any type of milk and shake it up again. |
| *Sweeten* | Eat a *wagashi*, or Japanese sweet, beforehand to prepare the palate for matcha's bitterness. | Add a sweetener (we prefer agave, stevia, maple syrup or coconut sugar) to your liking. |
| *Slurp* | Enjoy the matcha fairly quickly, as waiting longer will cause the foam to dissolve and particles to collect at the bottom of the bowl. Remember, matcha is a suspension tea. Japanese tradition dictates that it's totally okay to slurp the last, foamy sip. | Slurping never goes out of style. |

## *How to Make a Cold Matcha Drink*

Iced matcha lattes are now ubiquitous at matcha bars and many coffee shops. The only real secret to making a great drink—aside from starting with good matcha, of course—is to remember to always add the matcha to the liquid, not the other way around.

### *Iced Matcha Latte*

| | |
|---|---|
| *Fill* | Fill your shaking vessel—a cocktail or protein shaker, mason jar, or thermos—with water. A good rule of thumb is 1 to 2 grams (½ to 1 teaspoon) of matcha to 8 ounces of liquid to (depending on how strong you want it). The liquid can be entirely water, entirely milk, or a mixture of the two. |
| *Scoop/Sift* | Add the matcha to the liquid. It's best to sift the matcha first to prevent clumping, but we know that sometimes the extra minute can be too much. In that case, add the matcha directly to the water or milk. If you do sift the tea, do so directly into the vessel right before you shake to prevent clumping. |
| *Sweeten* | At this point, feel free to add sweetener of your choice. Agave tends to be the go-to choice of matcharistas. |
| *Shake* | Add a couple of ice cubes to the shaking vessel (which will help both chill and blend the mixture), seal the shaking vessel and shake, shake, shake Senora! |
| *Sip* | Pour or strain the latte over ice. |

# Chapter 5
# Cooking with Matcha

## Matcha in the Kitchen

Matcha lends an earthy, vegetal edge to food. This can pleasantly off-set sweetness in desserts, in which matcha is often used. Matcha can also lend its unique flavor to savory dishes, such as a bowl of oatmeal or a tempura batter or sauce, and add depth to an everyday vegetable dish, such as broccoli salad or glazed squash. However, according to our cooking-with-matcha expert, Ben Mims (who developed the recipes in this book), there is an art to cooking with matcha.

## Watch the Heat

A big word of caution: direct-heat cooking is matcha's enemy. (The tea, as Adele might say, can't handle the hot heat rising.) Don't add the powder directly to a hot pan—the matcha can stick to the bottom and burn immediately, which will accentuate the ingredient's bitterness. Instead, mix matcha into a dish after the heat is turned off. Also, because of the heat issue, don't use matcha as a dry rub for meat or for sautéing or roasting.

## Fat Is Key

The tea's flavor is carried very well by fat, be it butter, oil, cream, or chocolate, which is why it's an obvious ingredient for desserts and pastries. But adding matcha to baked goods—cakes, muffins, cookies, and so forth—can also dry them out. You can compensate by increasing the amount of fat in the dish.

## Break It Up

Matcha likes to clump in baking items. (It's very similar to baking with cocoa powder in this way.) You should always sift matcha through a fine-mesh sieve before using it. If the dish requires creaming butter, blend the matcha with the butter at the beginning to work out any lumps. Another way to avoid clumping is to blend the matcha with a little bit of liquid to make it into a paste before adding it to the recipe.

## Keep It Moist

Matcha works best in a damp environment. You can bake with it, but there has to be water or fat involved to keep it from getting too bitter.

## The Great Grade Debate

To use culinary grade or not to use culinary grade, that is the big question. Not all cooks agree on this topic. Many use culinary grade, noting that cooking with matcha of a higher ceremonial grade would compromise the tea because the powder isn't meant to be blended with other ingredients. They argue that using it can be very cost inefficient, like cooking with a fancy wine. Others prefer cooking with the good stuff. When developing the recipes in this book, Ben tried both styles of matcha in his recipes, and he usually had better results with a lesser-expensive ceremonial grade. And, unless you're making a huge batch of a recipe, the cost of a teaspoon or two of ceremonial grade won't break the bank. Our advice is to experiment with both styles to see what suits your taste best. And have fun!

# Matcha Granola
## with Cashews, Banana Chips, and Dates

*Serves 8*

The sweet, nutty flavors of dates, bananas, and coconut balance the earthy minerality of matcha in this granola. Serve it over yogurt, whole milk–even ice cream!–to add dairy richness, a perfect complement to matcha.

½ cup pure maple syrup

½ cup unsweetened applesauce

1 tablespoon matcha, sifted

1 tablespoon vegetable oil

3 cups rolled oats

1 cup raw cashews, roughly chopped

1 cup unsweetened flaked coconut

¼ cup granulated sugar

1 teaspoon kosher salt

1 cup pitted dates, roughly chopped

1½ cups banana chips, large pieces broken into bite-size pieces

Preheat the oven to 325°F. Whisk together the maple syrup, applesauce, matcha, and oil in a small bowl. Combine the oats, cashews, coconut, sugar, and salt in a large bowl and stir to mix evenly. Pour the syrup mixture over the oats and stir until evenly incorporated.

Spread the mixture on a rimmed baking sheet lined with parchment paper and bake, stirring every 15 minutes, until the granola is golden brown and toasted, about 45 minutes.

Once the granola comes out of the oven, stir once more, spread it out on the baking sheet, then let cool completely. Transfer the granola to a bowl and stir in the dates and banana chips. To store, place in a bag or storage container and keep at room temperature for up to 2 weeks.

# Matcha and Black Sesame Banana Bread

*Serves 8 to 10*

Superripe bananas make a sweet, creamy counterpoint for earthy matcha and toasty black sesame seeds in this breakfast loaf. Serve this banana bread in thick slices topped with almond butter, Greek yogurt, or your favorite jam–apricot pairs particularly well.

1¼ cups all-purpose flour

1 tablespoon matcha, sifted

¾ teaspoon baking soda

½ teaspoon kosher salt

3 tablespoons black sesame seeds

1 cup granulated sugar

½ cup vegetable oil

⅓ cup buttermilk

2 large eggs

1 teaspoon vanilla extract

3 very ripe bananas, mashed until smooth (about 1 cup)

Preheat the oven to 350°F. Line a 9-by-5-inch loaf pan with parchment paper.

Combine the flour, matcha, baking soda, and salt in a bowl and whisk to mix evenly. Set aside ½ teaspoon of the sesame seeds in a small bowl, then stir the remaining sesame seeds into the dry ingredients. In another bowl, whisk together the sugar, oil, buttermilk, eggs, vanilla, and bananas until smooth. Mix the wet and dry ingredients and stir until just combined.

Scrape the batter into the prepared pan, smooth the top, and sprinkle with the reserved sesame seeds. Bake until the top is golden brown and a toothpick inserted in the middle comes out clean, about 1 hour. (Check the bread after 45 minutes; if it is starting to brown too much on top, cover it loosely with a piece of foil.)

Transfer the pan to a rack and let cool for 20 minutes. Remove the bread from the mold and place on the rack. Let the bread cool completely before serving. Wrapped well in plastic wrap, the loaf will stay moist for up to 5 days.

# Matcha Japanese Milk Bread

*Serves 8 to 10*

Traditional Japanese milk bread, also called *shokupan*, is the perfect vehicle for matcha; the bread is creamy and sweet because of the milk and sugar it contains–a matcha latte in loaf form, if you will. The bread's characteristic texture comes from a "cooked" starter that acts to insulate and preserve the bread's moisture, while a simple overnight sourdough starter adds complexity and acidity to the sweet dough.

4½ cups all-purpose flour

1¼ teaspoons active dry yeast

1 cup whole milk

¼ cup granulated sugar

1½ tablespoons matcha, sifted

1 teaspoon kosher salt

4 tablespoons room-temperature unsalted butter, cut into 4 pieces, plus more for greasing the bowl and loaf pan

2 tablespoons heavy cream

Make the cooked starter: Combine ⅓ cup flour and ½ cup water in a small saucepan and whisk until smooth. Place the pan over medium heat and cook the slurry, whisking constantly, until thickened into a paste, about 1 to 2 minutes. Transfer the paste to a small bowl, cover with plastic wrap, and let cool completely to room temperature.

Make the raw starter: Combine ½ cup flour, ¼ teaspoon yeast, and ⅓ cup lukewarm water in a medium bowl and stir with a spoon to form a wet dough. Cover the bowl with plastic wrap, poke a hole in the top, and let the starter sit at room temperature for at least 8 hours or overnight.

Make the dough: Combine the milk and sugar in a small saucepan and bring to a simmer over medium heat, stirring to dissolve the sugar. Pour the mixture in a bowl and let cool until just warm to the touch. Stir in the remaining 1 teaspoon of yeast and let stand until foamy, about 10 minutes. Combine the remaining flour (3½ cups plus 2 tablespoons and 2 teaspoons), the matcha, and the salt in the bowl of a stand mixer fitted with a dough hook. Pour the yeast mixture into the flour along with the cooked and raw starters. Knead at medium speed for 6 minutes. With the mixer running, add the butter, 1 piece at a time, waiting until each piece is fully incorporated before adding the next piece (this will take 4 to 5 minutes). Transfer the dough to a lightly greased bowl, cover with plastic wrap, and let stand in a cold oven or microwave until doubled in size, about 1 to 1½ hours. Transfer to a lightly floured work surface and cut in half. Stretch each half into a 14-inch-long oval so the narrow ends of the ovals point toward and away from you. Fold the narrow ends of the ovals toward the center so they touch in the middle, forming rough squares. Working from one untouched side of a square, roll the dough, jelly roll–style, into a log; repeat with the other square. Transfer the logs to a lightly greased 9-by-5-inch loaf pan, positioning them each crosswise so their spiral ends are touching the long sides of the loaf pan. Cover the loaf pan loosely with plastic wrap and let stand in a cold oven or microwave until the dough just begins to peek over the edge of the pan, about 15 to 20 minutes.

Preheat the oven to 350°F. Uncover the loaf pan, brush the top of the dough with the cream, and bake until golden brown on top and an instant-read thermometer inserted in the center reads 185°F, about 40 to 45 minutes. Transfer the pan to a rack and let cool for 20 minutes. Remove the loaf from the pan and let cool completely before slicing. Well-wrapped in plastic wrap, it can keep for up to 5 days.

# Matcha and Chia-Seed Pancakes

*Serves 4*

These Dr. Suessian pancakes are packed with matcha and chia seeds, making them healthier than your average pancake and giving them a pleasant chewy texture. For a portable breakfast, sprinkle each pancake with Matcha Sugar (page 92) while it's warm, roll it up like a cigar, and dig into the warm pancakes and crunchy sugar while you're on the go. If you want to keep the pancakes warm as you finish cooking a batch, preheat your oven to 180°F and line a baking sheet with a clean kitchen towel. Place the pancakes in a single layer on the towel, cover with another kitchen towel, and keep warm in the oven for up to 30 minutes as you finish cooking the others.

2 tablespoons chia seeds

2 tablespoons matcha, sifted

1½ cups whole milk

3 tablespoons melted butter

½ teaspoon vanilla extract

2 large eggs

1¾ cups all-purpose flour

½ cup granulated sugar

1 tablespoon baking powder

¼ teaspoon baking soda

½ teaspoon kosher salt

Softened butter, for serving

Maple syrup, for serving

The night before, combine the chia seeds, matcha, and 1 cup of milk in a medium bowl. Cover with plastic wrap and refrigerate overnight.

The next morning, pour the matcha mixture into a bowl and whisk in the remaining ½ cup of milk and the butter, vanilla, and eggs. In a separate bowl, whisk together the flour, sugar, baking powder and soda, and salt. Combine the wet and dry ingredients and stir to make a thick batter. Let the batter stand for 5 minutes.

Heat a large nonstick skillet over medium heat. Ladle ¼ cup of the batter into the skillet, spreading it into a 4-inch round, and cook until bubbles break the surface of the pancake and the underside is golden brown, about 1 minute. Flip the pancake with a spatula and cook until the batter is cooked through on the second side, about 45 seconds. Repeat with the remaining batter. Serve the pancakes with butter and maple syrup.

# No-Bake Matcha Energy Bars

*Makes about 30 bars*

A DIY alternative to granola or store-bought energy bars, the dried fruit and nuts in these treats combined with energizing matcha make for a nutritious snack or breakfast bar. Be careful when processing the fruits and nuts together; don't let them turn into a paste, or the nuts' oils will separate too much from the rest of the mixture, making the bars feel greasy.

1 cup dried apricots

1 cup pitted dates

1 cup walnuts

1 cup raw cashews

1 tablespoon matcha, sifted

¼ teaspoon kosher salt

1 cup goji berries or golden raisins

½ cup roasted and salted sunflower seeds

Line an 8-inch square baking pan with parchment paper, letting the paper hang over two of the sides.

Combine the apricots, dates, walnuts, cashews, matcha, and salt in a food processor and pulse until all the ingredients are finely chopped and evenly mixed. Add the goji berries and sunflower seeds and pulse just enough to combine.

Scrape the mixture into the prepared pan and flatten evenly over the bottom. Refrigerate until set, at least 1 hour.

Use the parchment paper to transfer the flattened mixture onto a cutting board, then cut into 1-inch squares or triangles. Wrap each square in plastic wrap or seal them in a plastic bag. The bars will keep for up to 2 weeks in the refrigerator.

# Carrot and Olive-Oil Cake
## with Matcha-Cream Frosting

*Serves 10 to 12*

Mixed into a sweet cream frosting, matcha adds an extra layer of flavor to a classic carrot cake, sans all the overwhelming spices typically added to the cake batter. Olive oil adds complexity to the cake, echoing the "green" flavor of the matcha in the frosting. Don't be tempted to use fancy extra-virgin olive oil; its flavor will overwhelm the matcha.

### For the cake:

¾ cup olive oil, plus more for greasing the pans

2 cups all-purpose flour, plus more for dusting

2 teaspoons baking powder

2 teaspoons baking soda

½ teaspoon kosher salt

1½ cups granulated sugar

½ cup buttermilk

2 teaspoons vanilla extract

4 large eggs

4 cups finely grated carrots

### For the frosting:

1½ cups granulated sugar

⅓ cup all-purpose flour

2 tablespoons matcha, sifted

½ teaspoon kosher salt

1½ cups whole milk

1½ cups (3 sticks) unsalted butter, at room temperature

Preheat the oven to 350°F. Lightly grease the insides of two 9-inch round cake pans with olive oil, line with parchment-paper rounds, oil the parchment, and then dust the pan with flour, tapping out the excess.

Make the cake: Combine the flour, baking powder and soda, and salt in a large bowl and whisk to combine. In a medium bowl, whisk the olive oil, sugar, buttermilk, vanilla, and eggs until smooth. Pour the wet ingredients over the dry ingredients and whisk just until combined. Stir in the carrots, then divide the batter between the prepared pans, smoothing their tops. Bake until golden brown on top and a toothpick inserted in the middle of each comes out with no crumbs attached, about 25 to 30 minutes. Transfer the pans to a wire rack and let cool completely. Invert the cakes on the rack and remove the pans and parchment rounds.

Make the frosting: Combine the sugar, flour, matcha, and salt in a medium saucepan and whisk until evenly combined. Stir in the milk, then place the pan over medium-high heat and bring to a boil, whisking constantly. Once the mixture boils, continue cooking and whisking until the mixture forms a very thick paste, about 5 minutes (this amount of time also cooks off the raw flour taste in the mixture). Remove the pan from the heat and scrape the paste into a bowl. Cover the bowl with plastic wrap and let cool completely to room temperature.

Place the butter in the bowl of a stand mixer fitted with a paddle attachment and beat at medium speed until fluffy, about 2 minutes. Add one-third of the paste, beat until smooth, then add another one-third of the paste, beating again until smooth. Add the remaining paste, beat until smooth, and increase the speed to high and beat until light and fluffy, about 3 minutes.

Place 1 cake on a cake stand and spread about 1 cup of the frosting over the top. Top with the other cake and spread the remaining frosting over the top and sides of both cakes. Refrigerate until the frosting is firm, at least 1 hour, before serving.

# Matcha Rice Pudding
## with Orange Jam

*Serves 6*

Like horchata or a rice-thickened latte, this pudding is the perfect showcase for matcha and makes a great creamy dessert–hot or cold. The fresh orange segments tossed with marmalade brighten the rich pudding; feel free to use blood oranges, Cara Cara, mandarins, or any other orange-like citrus that's in season.

1 cup basmati or jasmine rice

1 teaspoon kosher salt

4 cups half-and-half

1 cup granulated sugar

1 tablespoon plus 1 teaspoon matcha, sifted

2 oranges

¼ cup orange marmalade

Combine the rice, salt, and 2 cups of water in a medium saucepan and bring to a boil, stirring occasionally. Reduce the heat to low, cover, and cook, stirring occasionally, until all the water is absorbed, about 8 to 10 minutes. Stir in the half-and-half, sugar, and matcha and return to a boil. Reduce the heat to low and cook, stirring until the rice is cooked through and the pudding is thickened, about 16 to 18 minutes. Remove the pan from the heat, cover, and keep warm.

Using a sharp knife, cut away the peel and white pith from the oranges. Working over a bowl, cut between the membranes to release the orange segments into the bowl. Squeeze the juice from the orange membranes into the bowl. Fish out the segments, place them on a cutting board, and cut them into ½-inch pieces. Add the marmalade to the bowl and whisk vigorously until evenly combined. Return the chopped segments to the bowl and stir to combine.

Divide the pudding among serving bowls, top each with a dollop of the oranges and marmalade, and serve.

# Matcha Tres Leches Cake
## with Toasted Coconut

*Serves 12*

Coconut milk adds a unique twist to the traditional tres leches, while matcha balances the milk's richness and tints the dessert a beautiful pastel green. Make this cake a day before you plan to serve it so it has ample time to soak up all the milk.

Unsalted butter or coconut oil, for greasing the pan

2 cups all-purpose flour, plus more for dusting the pan

1 tablespoon plus 1 teaspoon baking powder

1 tablespoon matcha, sifted

1 teaspoon kosher salt

6 large eggs, separated

1½ cups granulated sugar

½ cup whole milk

1 cup heavy cream

One 14-ounce can sweetened condensed milk

One 13.5-ounce can unsweetened coconut milk

Toasted coconut flakes, for serving

Preheat the oven to 325°F. Lightly grease a 9-by-13-inch metal baking pan with butter and dust with flour, tapping out the excess.

Combine the flour, baking powder, matcha, and salt in a medium bowl and whisk until evenly mixed. Place the egg whites in the bowl of a stand mixer fitted with the whisk attachment and beat at medium-high speed until soft peaks form. With the machine running, slowly pour in the sugar and continue whisking until stiff peaks form. Add the egg yolks and milk, whisk at low speed until smooth, and then remove the bowl from the mixer. Using a large rubber spatula, fold in the dry ingredients until just combined. Spread the batter in the prepared baking pan and smooth the top. Bake until lightly browned on top and a toothpick inserted in the middle comes out clean, about 25 to 30 minutes. Leave the cake in the pan and transfer to a wire rack to let cool completely.

Meanwhile, whisk together the cream, sweetened condensed milk, and unsweetened coconut milk in a bowl until smooth. Once the cake is cool, trim the lightly browned top away with a serrated knife to expose the cake inside. Poke vertically oriented holes in the cake using a wooden skewer; the cake should be completely covered with holes. (You want there to be a hole every ¼ inch or so). Then slowly pour the milk mixture over the cake. (It will look like the cake is drowning in liquid.) Wrap the pan in plastic wrap and refrigerate until the cake absorbs all of the milk, at least 2 hours, or preferably overnight.

Cut the cake into squares and serve with toasted coconut flakes sprinkled on top.

# Matcha Mousse

*Serves 8*

Similar in flavor and texture to no-bake cheesecake filling, this mousse comes together in a couple of minutes–and without you having to cook a thing! The matcha is a perfect foil for the rich, tangy sour cream and cream cheese. Serve the mousse with a bright raspberry or apricot jam, if you'd like, to reduce its richness and add a little color.

1 cup granulated sugar

2 tablespoons matcha, sifted

½ teaspoon kosher salt

8 ounces cream cheese, softened

1 cup sour cream

2 cups heavy cream, chilled

Combine the sugar, matcha, and salt in a food processor and pulse to combine. Add the cream cheese and sour cream and process until very smooth, at least 1 minute. Scrape the matcha cream into a medium bowl.

In a large bowl, beat the heavy cream to stiff peaks. Fold half the whipped cream into the matcha cream until blended. Spoon the mousse into glasses and refrigerate for at least 2 hours, or overnight, along with the remaining whipped cream.

Serve the mousse chilled and topped with the whipped cream.

## Ask the Expert:

*My first matcha experience:*

Probably like many, my first taste of matcha came in the form of green tea ice cream at the end of a Japanese bento-box meal as a kid. I never remember it actually being called matcha, though.

*Where I source my matcha:*

I've used a couple brands in the past, like Harney & Sons. Since most of my matcha preparations use dairy and other ingredients, I stick with the culinary grade.

*Matcha obstacles:*

If I'm making a recipe that requires creaming butter, I will put the powder in with the butter at the beginning to work out any lumps. If I'm making a mousse, I like to blend the matcha with a little warm cream and give it a good whisk before adding it to the rest of my mousse base.

*Home cooking advice:*

Start by buying matcha from a reputable source, like a good Japanese grocer or high-end tea purveyor, online or brick and mortar. Look for the culinary-grade matcha. Once you have it, store it in the freezer between uses to retain its vibrant color.

*Jen Yee*
*New York City–based pastry chef, formerly of Lafayette and SHO Shaun Hergatt*

# Matcha Meringue Tart

*Serves 8*

Matcha and coconut are a natural pairing. The chewy macaroon-like coconut crust balances the rich matcha pudding in this dessert, and a cloud of fluffy toasted meringue lightens things up. It's important to cover the filling with plastic wrap as soon as you pour it into the crust; then, once you've made the meringue, spread it on top of the filling while both are still warm. The plastic wrap prevents the filling from cooling; if it cools or forms a skin, the meringue will have a hard time sticking to it.

**For the crust:**

2 tablespoons coconut oil, plus more for greasing the pan

2 cups unsweetened shredded coconut (7 ounces)

⅓ cup granulated sugar

½ teaspoon kosher salt

1 egg white

**For the filling:**

½ cup granulated sugar

¼ cup cornstarch

1 tablespoon matcha, sifted

½ teaspoon kosher salt

5 large egg yolks

2 cups whole milk

2 tablespoons unsalted butter, cut into ½-inch cubes

½ teaspoon vanilla extract

**For the meringue:**

1¼ cups granulated sugar

1 tablespoon cornstarch

5 large egg whites

1 teaspoon vanilla extract

Make the crust: Preheat the oven to 325°F and lightly grease a 9½-inch tart pan with coconut oil. Combine the 2 tablespoons coconut oil, shredded coconut, sugar, salt, and egg white in a medium bowl and mix with your hands until a stiff dough forms. Press the coconut mixture evenly into the bottom and up the sides of the tart pan, creating a ¼-inch thick wall and base. Bake until golden brown and set, about 25 to 30 minutes. Transfer to a rack and let cool completely.

Make the filling: Combine the sugar, cornstarch, matcha, and salt in a medium saucepan and stir to mix evenly. Add the yolks and stir until smooth. Stir in the milk and bring to a simmer over medium heat, stirring constantly. Cook the custard, stirring often, until it thickens and is bubbling, about 5 to 7 minutes. Remove the pan from the heat and stir in the butter and vanilla until smooth. Scrape the pudding into the cooled tart crust and smooth the top. Place a sheet of plastic wrap directly on the surface of the pudding (do not refrigerate).

Make the meringue (immediately!): Combine the sugar, cornstarch, and egg whites in the bowl of a stand mixer fitted with the whisk attachment. Place the bowl over a small saucepan of simmering water, stirring constantly, until the sugar dissolves and the mixture is warm to the touch (an instant-read thermometer should read no higher than 140°F).

Remove the bowl from the pan, attach it to the stand mixer, and beat the meringue at medium-high speed until glossy and fluffy, about 3 minutes. Beat in the vanilla and then spread the meringue evenly onto the warm tart filling; leave about ½ inch of the filling exposed around the edge. Brown the outside of the meringue using a broiler or kitchen torch, and then let the pie cool completely to set the filling before serving.

# Salted Matcha Ice Cream

*Makes 5 cups*

Matcha, like salt, can add savoriness to ice cream (think salted caramel). This recipe calls for more egg yolks than necessary to set the custard, but it's those extra yolks that create the rich, smooth, velvety texture of this ice cream. When cooking the custard, cook it gently and stir constantly to avoid having any egg scrambling on the bottom of the pan. If you desire precision and accuracy, the custard is ready when an instant-read thermometer inserted in it reads 180°F.

4 large egg yolks

1 cup sugar

1 tablespoon matcha, sifted

½ teaspoon kosher salt

2 cups whole milk

1 cup heavy cream

½ teaspoon vanilla extract

1½ teaspoons flaky sea salt

Place the egg yolks in a small saucepan and whisk to combine. Add ¼ cup of the sugar and whisk until combined with the yolks. Repeat, adding ¼ cup sugar at a time and whisking until the mixture forms a thick paste; stir in the matcha and salt until smooth.

Stir in the milk, then place the pan over medium heat. Cook the custard, stirring constantly with a wooden spoon, until it thickens slightly and coats the back of the spoon (or reaches 180°F on an instant-read thermometer), about 8 to 12 minutes. Pour the custard through a fine-mesh sieve into a bowl, stir in the cream and vanilla, and let cool completely. Refrigerate the custard until chilled, at least 4 hours.

Pour the chilled custard into an ice cream maker and churn according to the manufacturer's instructions. During the last 10 seconds of churning, add the flaky sea salt so that it mixes evenly into the ice cream but doesn't dissolve. Scrape the ice cream into a container and freeze until solid, at least 4 hours, before serving.

# Berries with Matcha Sugar and Cream

*Serves 6 to 8*

Mixing with sugar is one of the simplest ways to add matcha to a dessert. In this dish, the matcha lends its unique flavor to a mix of fresh berries, balancing their tartness and coating them in a sweet matcha-flavored syrup as they macerate. If you've already made Matcha Sugar (age 92), simply substitute it for the granulated sugar and omit the matcha.

¼ cup plus 2 tablespoons granulated sugar

1 tablespoon matcha, sifted

1 pound strawberries, hulled and cut crosswise into ¼-inch-thick rounds (halved or left whole if small)

6 ounces blackberries

6 ounces raspberries

1 cup heavy cream, chilled

Combine the sugar and matcha in a small bowl and whisk to combine. In a large bowl, combine the strawberries, blackberries, raspberries, and ¼ cup of the matcha-sugar mixture and toss to combine. Let the mixture stand, tossing once or twice more, until the sugar has dissolved and the fruit has released its juices, about 20 minutes.

Meanwhile, whisk the cream and remaining 2 tablespoons of the matcha-sugar mixture in a large bowl until stiff peaks form. Divide the berries among bowls and dollop with the matcha whipped cream, if using.

## Ask the Expert:

*My first matcha experience:*

The first time I made matcha ice cream, I was trying to bring raspberries into a dessert. We were getting raspberries into early fall. I paired them with the earthiness of the green tea, because it really complemented the raspberries, but it tasted like they belonged in the fall desert. The contrast of the bright green with the raspberry, and all the flavors, were really good.

*Matcha obstacles:*

One way to get it a little smoother is if you stir it with sugar or powdered sugar. That helps break apart the lumps. Also, if it gets too hot, it gets bitter.

*Favorite matcha pairings:*

I think it pairs really well with coconut or anything with coconut milk. It goes really well with chocolate. I've been doing a gelato—a grown-up version of cookies and cream: matcha gelato with dark chocolate cookies swirled through. It's fun to do matcha mint chip; I'm able to get the natural green "mint" color without using green food coloring.

**Mathew Rice**
*Chicago-based pastry chef, formerly of*
*Girl & the Goat and Little Goat Diner*

# Matcha and Honeydew Melon Granita

*Serves 8*

Though seemingly light in flavor, honeydew melon stands up to matcha in this creamy granita, which can be served as a simple dessert or an afternoon pick-me-up. If you'd prefer to buy precut honeydew melon cubes, you'll need to buy 1¾ pounds (about three 10-ounce packs, minus a cube or two for snacking).

½ honeydew melon (about 2¼ pounds), peeled and seeded

1 cup sugar

2 tablespoons fresh lemon juice

2 teaspoons matcha, sifted

½ teaspoon kosher salt

Place the melon in a blender and puree until smooth. You should have 4 cups of puree; if not, add enough water to make 4 cups. Add the sugar, lemon juice, matcha, and salt and puree until the sugar dissolves, at least 1 minute.

Pour the mixture into a 9-by-13-inch baking pan and place in the freezer until the mixture is the consistency of shaved ice, about 4 hours. Scrape and stir the mixture thoroughly every hour or so to prevent it from freezing into a solid mass. Spoon the granita into chilled bowls and serve.

# *Matcha and White Chocolate Bark* *with Pistachios*

*Serves 12 to 16*

This whimsical and beautiful white chocolate bark comes together in just a couple of minutes. Feel free to use any buttery nuts–cashews, Brazil nuts, or macadamia nuts–instead of pistachios. Chopped dried fruits such as apricots, dates, and cherries complement the matcha and chocolate as well.

1 pound high-quality white chocolate, finely chopped

2 teaspoons matcha, sifted

⅓ cup roasted, salted pistachios, roughly chopped

Matcha Salt (page 100), optional

Place the white chocolate in a heatproof bowl. Bring 1 inch of water to a simmer in a small saucepan, then place the bowl of chocolate over it and stir until the chocolate is almost completely melted. Remove the bowl from the pan and stir until smooth and all the chocolate pieces have melted.

Line a baking sheet with foil or wax paper, then pour all but about ⅓ cup of the white chocolate onto the sheet, spreading it into a rough 8-by-13-inch rectangle. Add the matcha to the remaining white chocolate in the bowl and stir until smooth. Using a spoon, drizzle the matcha chocolate over the plain white chocolate. Sprinkle the pistachios evenly over the chocolate and top with Matcha Salt, if you like, or plain flaky sea salt.

Refrigerate the bark until firm, about 1 hour, and then break into 2-inch pieces to serve. Refrigerate the bark stacked in layers and separated by paper towels in a plastic container for up to 2 weeks.

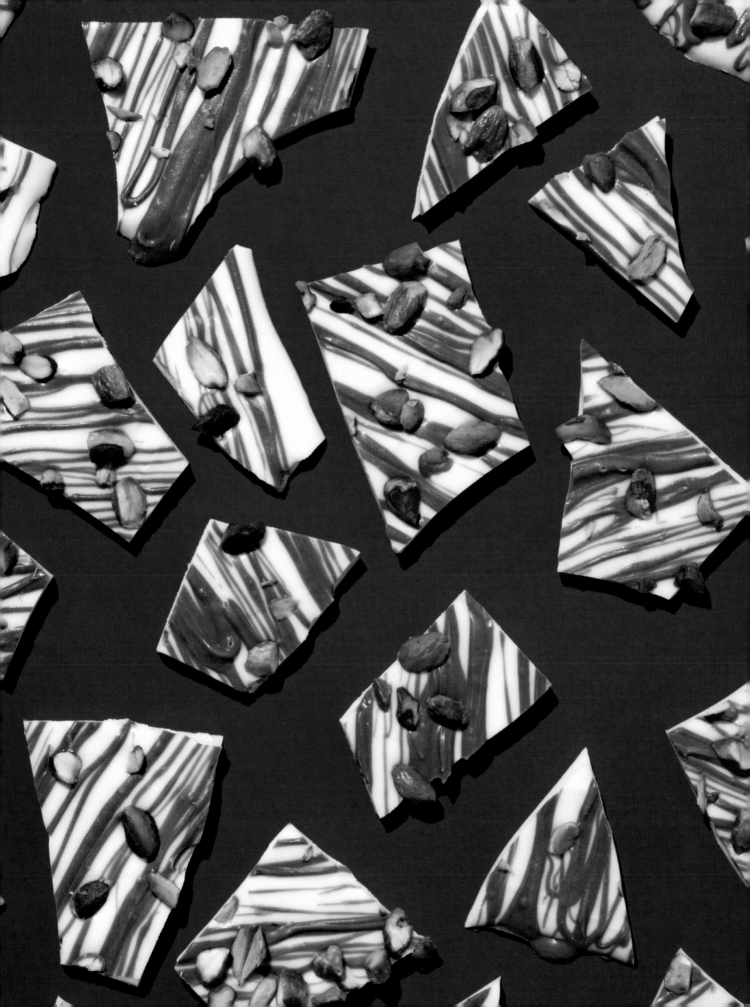

# Matcha-Ginger Shortbread

*Makes 8 cookies*

This buttery shortbread is the perfect canvas for matcha. It lends the rich cookies a touch of earthy sweetness that is balanced by the spicy candied-ginger chunks. Mixing the dough for 10 minutes in a mixer may seem unorthodox, but it's the difference between crisp, flaky cookies and crumbly ones that don't hold their shape.

⅓ cup granulated sugar

1 teaspoon matcha, sifted

¼ teaspoon kosher salt

8 tablespoons (1 stick) unsalted butter, at room temperature

1½ cups all-purpose flour

3 tablespoons finely chopped candied ginger

Preheat the oven to 325°F. Line the bottom of an 8-inch round cake pan with a circle of parchment paper.

Combine the sugar, matcha, and salt in the bowl of a stand mixer fitted with the paddle attachment. Add the butter and mix at medium-low speed until smooth, about 1 minute. Add the flour and mix until just combined. Once the dough forms crumbles, continue mixing at low speed for 10 minutes (this amount of time helps develop gluten, which you want in order to create shortbread's characteristic brittle texture). Add 2 tablespoons of candied ginger and mix until evenly combined.

Transfer the dough to the prepared pan and press evenly into the bottom. Using a paring knife, score the dough into 8 wedges. Using the tines of a form, prick the dough all over, being careful to stay within the lines of the wedges. Sprinkle the remaining 1 tablespoon of candied ginger evenly over the top.

Bake until cooked through and the lightest golden brown at the edges, about 45 minutes. Transfer the pan to a wire rack and cut along the score lines to separate the wedges while the shortbread is hot. Let the shortbread cool completely in the pan, then gently invert to remove the wedges.

# Matcha Marble-Cream Cookies

*Makes about 4 dozen*

Rolling two different doughs–one made with matcha, one without–together creates cookies that are all unique in appearance but equal in their sweet, matcha-y flavor. An hour and a half may seem like an unnecessarily long time to chill the dough balls, but they need to be well chilled or else they'll spread too much on the baking sheets. Don't let the cookies cool for longer than 1 minute on the baking sheet, or else they may stick.

1¾ cups plus 3 tablespoons all-purpose flour

1½ teaspoons cream of tartar

½ teaspoon baking soda

½ teaspoon kosher salt

1 tablespoon matcha, sifted

1 cup granulated sugar

12 tablespoons (1½ sticks) unsalted butter, at room temperature

½ teaspoon vanilla extract

2 large eggs

Whisk together 1 cup flour, ¾ teaspoon cream of tartar, ¼ teaspoon baking soda, and ¼ teaspoon salt in a medium bowl. In another medium bowl, stir together the matcha and the remaining ¾ cup plus 3 tablespoons flour, ¾ teaspoon cream of tartar, ¼ teaspoon baking soda, and ¼ teaspoon salt.

In the bowl of a stand mixer fitted with a whisk attachment, beat the sugar, butter, and vanilla at medium speed until pale and fluffy, about 3 minutes. Add the eggs, one at a time, beating well after each addition. Spoon half of the butter mixture into the matcha mixture, and spoon the remaining butter mixture into the plain flour mixture. Beat the plain batter until just combined, then beat the matcha batter until just combined. Refrigerate both batters for 30 minutes.

Drop level tablespoonfuls of plain dough onto a foil-lined baking sheet. Top each with 1 tablespoon of the matcha dough, and then roll the two together into a ball; chill the balls for 1 hour.

Preheat the oven to 350°F. Evenly space 9 balls on an ungreased and unlined baking sheet and bake until the edges are lightly browned, about 14 minutes. Let the cookies cool for 1 minute on the baking sheets, and then transfer them to wire racks to cool completely.

# Matcha Milk Jam

*Makes ¾ cup*

Traditional milk jam, called *kaya* in Indonesia, is colored green with pandan leaves, a fragrant native plant. In this milk jam, matcha plays that role in addition to adding its flavor to the rich, egg-thickened custard sauce, which can be spread over toast, drizzled over fresh fruit, or used as a topping for a bowl of oatmeal or granola. It's very addictive stuff, so once you've had your first taste don't be shy about doubling or tripling this recipe.

6 egg yolks

½ cup granulated sugar

1 tablespoon matcha, sifted

¼ teaspoon kosher salt

¾ cup heavy cream

¼ teaspoon vanilla extract

Combine the egg yolks, sugar, matcha, and salt in a small saucepan and whisk until evenly mixed. Stir in the cream, place over medium heat, and cook, stirring until the mixture thickens on the back of the spoon, about 8 to 10 minutes. Remove the pan from the heat, stir in the vanilla, and scrape the mixture into a bowl. Let the jam cool to room temperature, then transfer it to a jar and seal. Refrigerate for up to 2 weeks.

# Matcha Marshmallows

*Makes 3 dozen*

Matcha makes awesome marshmallows because its bitter flavor tames the confection's typical cloying sweetness. Roast these marshmallows for s'mores made with white chocolate, drop them into a mug of Hot Matcha and White Chocolate (page 158), or melt them down to use for a matcha variation on crisped-rice cereal treats.

3 (¼-ounce) packets unflavored powdered gelatin

2 tablespoons plus 1 teaspoon matcha, sifted

1½ cups sugar

1 cup light corn syrup

½ teaspoon kosher salt

1 teaspoon vanilla extract

¼ cup confectioners' sugar

¼ cup cornstarch

Nonstick spray

Place the gelatin and ½ cup cold water into the bowl of a stand mixer fitted with a whisk attachment and let stand for at least 5 minutes, then add 2 tablespoons matcha on top.

In a small saucepan, combine the sugar, corn syrup, salt, and ½ cup water. Place the pan over medium-high heat, cover, and allow the mixture to cook for 3 to 4 minutes. Uncover the pan, attach a candy thermometer to its side, and continue to cook until the mixture reaches 240°F, about 7 to 8 minutes.

Remove the pan from the heat, turn the mixer to low speed and, while the mixer is running, slowly pour the sugar syrup down the side of the bowl into the gelatin and matcha. Once you have added all of the syrup, increase the speed to high. Continue to whip until the mixture becomes very thick and is lukewarm, about 12 minutes; add the vanilla during the last minute of whipping.

While the mixture is whipping, combine the remaining 1 teaspoon matcha, confectioners' sugar, and cornstarch in a small bowl. Lightly spray a 9-by-13-inch metal baking pan with nonstick cooking spray, line with a sheet of parchment paper, and spray the parchment. Using a sieve, dust the pan with some of the cornstarch mixture to evenly coat it; reserve the rest.

When ready, use a lightly greased rubber spatula to pour and spread the marshmallow mixture evenly into the prepared pan. Dust the top with enough of the remaining sugar and cornstarch mixture to lightly cover the mixture; reserve the rest. Allow the marshmallows to set, uncovered, for at least 6 hours or overnight.

Turn the marshmallow mixture out of the pan onto a cutting board dusted with some of the cornstarch mixture, dust the marshmallow mixture with more cornstarch mixture, and then cut the marshmallow mixture into 1½-inch squares using a chef's knife or pizza cutter dusted with the cornstarch mixture. Once cut, lightly dust all sides of each marshmallow with the remaining cornstarch mixture. Store in an airtight container for up to 3 weeks.

# Matcha Sugar

*Makes about 1 cup*

Keep this matcha-flavored sugar around for stirring into yogurt, adding to smoothies, or dusting over sugar cookies during the holidays. Turbinado sugar makes for a crunchier alternative, though the matcha's color won't be as vibrant with darker sugars.

1 cup granulated sugar

3 tablespoons matcha, sifted

Combine the sugar and matcha in a bowl until evenly mixed. Transfer to a container and keep for up to 6 months.

# Matcha-Oatmeal Breakfast Bowl

*Serves 4*

Matcha's lean flavor plays well with creamy oatmeal for a savory twist on the breakfast bowl of oats, topped with rich avocado and a runny egg and spiked with fresh chiles. You can make the oatmeal up to an hour before you're ready to serve; keep it warm until the eggs are poached, then assemble.

4 cups chicken broth or water

2 teaspoons kosher salt

2 cups quick-cooking steel-cut oats

2 tablespoons matcha, sifted

4 large eggs

1 avocado, cut into quarters and thinly sliced crosswise

1 lemon, cut into 4 wedges

Flaky sea salt

1 red Fresno chile or jalapeño (or 2 red Thai chiles), stemmed and thinly sliced

Bring the broth (or water) and salt to a boil in a medium saucepan. Stir in the oats; reduce the heat to maintain a gentle simmer; and cook, stirring occasionally, until the oats are tender and thickened, about 20 minutes.

Remove the pan from the heat. In a small bowl, stir a spoonful of the oatmeal's starchy liquid into the matcha until smooth. Then stir the matcha mixture into the oatmeal until evenly dispersed. Cover the oats to keep them warm.

Fill a large skillet halfway with water and bring to a gentle simmer. Crack each egg into a small bowl, then lower each one into the simmering water. Cook, swirling the water around each egg occasionally, until the whites are set and the yolks are still runny, about 2 to 3 minutes. Using a slotted spoon, lift each egg from the water and transfer to paper towels to drain.

Divide the oats among 4 bowls, then top each serving with an egg and ¼ of the avocado. Squeeze a lemon wedge over each portion of avocado, and then sprinkle the avocado and egg with sea salt. Sprinkle each bowl with sliced chiles, and serve immediately.

# Matcha and Citrus Hummus

*Makes 4 cups*

Matcha plays off the nuttiness of the chickpeas and tahini particularly well in this speedy hummus. Any vegetables can be used as crudités, but green ones, such as celery, green beans, and broccoli, pair especially well with the "green" flavor of the matcha. If you have the patience, remove the skins from the chickpeas before blending for a smoother hummus.

¼ cup fresh lemon juice

¼ cup fresh orange juice

1 garlic clove, roughly chopped

Two 15-ounce cans (3 cups) chickpeas, drained and rinsed

¾ cup (6 ounces) tahini

2 teaspoons matcha, sifted

1½ teaspoons kosher salt

1 tablespoon finely chopped flat-leaf parsley

Olive oil, for drizzling

Crudités and pita chips, for serving

Combine the lemon and orange juices and garlic in a food processor and blend until smooth. Add the chickpeas, tahini, matcha, salt, and ½ cup cold water and puree until velvety smooth, at least 5 minutes.

Spread the hummus on the bottom of a shallow bowl, sprinkle with the parsley, and drizzle with olive oil. Serve the hummus with crudités and pita chips. Store the hummus in an airtight container for up to 1 week.

# Matcha-Marinated Tomatoes

*Serves 6 to 8*

Matcha adds a sweet earthiness to fresh tomatoes in this bright salad speckled with sweet tarragon and sharp chives. Use the "roll cut" method to cut the large tomatoes into attractive pieces: Cut a bite-size chunk of tomato from one side, rotate the tomato 90 degrees along the cutting board, then cut again; repeat until you have lots of irregular and angled pieces.

1½ pounds cherry tomatoes, halved

¼ cup vegetable oil

3 tablespoons white wine vinegar

1½ teaspoons matcha, sifted

1 small shallot, thinly sliced lengthwise

Kosher salt

1½ pounds heirloom tomatoes, cored and cut into 2-inch chunks

¼ cup loosely packed tarragon leaves

Freshly cracked black pepper

2 tablespoons coarsely chopped chives

Flaky sea salt

In a large bowl, toss the cherry tomatoes with the oil, vinegar, matcha, and shallot. Season with salt and let stand, about 20 minutes to marry the flavors, stirring every 5 minutes.

Add the heirloom tomatoes and tarragon and toss to combine. Spread on a platter and season with pepper. Sprinkle the tomatoes with chives and sea salt before serving.

### Ask the Expert:

*My first matcha experience:*

When I was a kid, I'd eat green tea ice cream when I went out for sushi. The best way I could describe it when I was young is it had a really subtle cocoa flavor.

*What I've made with matcha:*

Matcha petit fours, cake, and truffles. I've done matcha salad dressings, butter, and ice cream.

*What I don't love matcha with:*

Meat. Mostly matcha and dairy or matcha and nonanimal fats go really well together.

*Matcha is great in pastries because of:*

The color! It stops people in their tracks. It feels unnatural. The color is so intense and vibrant. I think for chefs, there is always a thing of getting natural color so you aren't living in a world of beige or brown.

*Valerie Gordon*
*Owner of Valerie Confections, Los Angeles*

# Matcha-Glazed Squash
## with Crunchy Quinoa

*Serves 4*

This dish is inspired by a traditional Japanese preparation, in which large chunks of squash are steamed in a skillet with water, butter, and sugar until tender and coated in a glaze. Matcha colors the glaze and adds a bitter tang while fried quinoa, charred and sliced scallions, and roasted pepitas add crunch and complexity. If you like, you can just make the squash and skip the accompaniments; the dish will still taste great.

4 tablespoons unsalted butter

1 tablespoon granulated sugar

1 teaspoon kosher salt, plus more

1 small kabocha, butternut, or acorn squash (about 2½ pounds)—peeled, seeded and cut into 1½-inch pieces

1 teaspoon matcha, sifted

½ cup quinoa

2 scallions, trimmed and halved crosswise

Freshly ground black pepper

2 tablespoons roasted, salted pepitas (pumpkin seeds)

Combine 2 tablespoons butter, the sugar, 1 teaspoon salt, the squash, and ½ cup water in a large nonstick skillet or wok and bring to a boil over high heat. Reduce the heat to medium and cover, stirring occasionally until the squash is tender, about 10 to 12 minutes. Stir in the matcha, then transfer the squash to a bowl and keep warm. Wipe the skillet clean and reserve.

Bring a medium saucepan of water to a boil and add the quinoa, stirring occasionally until tender, about 10 minutes. Drain the quinoa, spread on a baking sheet, and let cool completely.

Heat the remaining 2 tablespoons butter in the large nonstick skillet over medium-high heat. Add the cooled quinoa, spread it out in a single layer and cook, stirring occasionally, until fried crisp, about 12 to 15 minutes. Transfer the quinoa to paper towels and let cool.

Wipe the skillet clean and return it to high heat. Add the scallions and cook, turning once halfway through, until they are lightly blackened on the outside and tender, about 5 minutes. Transfer the scallions to a cutting board and let cool. Coarsely chop the halved scallions and season with salt and pepper.

Divide the squash among 4 small bowls and top each with the fried quinoa, scallions, and pepitas before serving.

# Shaved Broccoli
## with Matcha-Honey Vinaigrette and Manchego

*Serves 4 to 6*

Matcha enhances the smoky, bitter flavor of lightly charred broccoli in this simple side dish. For an attractive presentation, and to more evenly disperse the nutty manchego cheese, shave it over the top of the broccoli with a Microplane grater.

2 heads broccoli (about 1 pound), stalks peeled

3 tablespoons vegetable oil

Kosher salt and freshly ground black pepper

1 teaspoon matcha, sifted

2 teaspoons honey

2 teaspoons fresh lemon juice

1 ounce manchego cheese

Using a mandoline or chef's knife, thinly slice the broccoli stalks on a bias until you reach the base of the florets. Turn the florets on their side and continue shaving until you've used the entire broccoli heads.

Heat 2 tablespoons oil in a large nonstick skillet over high heat. Add the shaved broccoli, season with salt and pepper, and toss to combine with the oil. Cook, undisturbed, until the bottom of the broccoli starts to caramelize, about 4 minutes. Toss the broccoli again and continue cooking, stirring and tossing occasionally, until the broccoli is tender and lightly caramelized all over, about 4 minutes longer. Spread the broccoli in a single layer on a platter.

In a small bowl, whisk the remaining 1 tablespoon oil with the matcha until smooth, then stir in the honey and lemon juice. Season the dressing with salt, then drizzle it over the broccoli and finely grate the manchego over the top.

# Vegan Matcha and Cashew Soup

*Serves 4 to 6*

Though milk is the standard complement to matcha, other creamy foods work just as well, including raw cashews and coconut cream, both of which add body and richness to this easy vegan soup. Buy organic coconut milk without stabilizers so you can easily skim the natural "cream," or fat, that has risen to the top of the can. Use the leftover coconut milk in smoothies, milk shakes–or in a coconut matcha latte!

6 cups vegetable broth

1½ cups raw cashews

One 13.5-ounce can unsweetened coconut milk, chilled (do not shake the can)

1 tablespoon matcha, sifted

¼ cup coconut oil

1 small shallot, thinly sliced lengthwise

Kosher salt and freshly ground pepper

Chopped chives, for garnish

Bring the broth and cashews to a boil in a medium saucepan. Meanwhile, open the can of coconut milk and skim off the thick cream at the top (reserve the coconut milk for another use). Stir the cream into the soup and continue cooking, stirring occasionally, until the cashews are tender, about 10 minutes. Pour the soup into a blender, add the matcha, and blend until very smooth, at least 1 minute.

Meanwhile, combine the coconut oil and sliced shallot in a small skillet. Cook over high heat, stirring occasionally, until the shallots start frying and turn golden brown, about 5 minutes. Using a slotted spoon, transfer the shallots to paper towels to drain; discard the coconut oil or save for another use.

Season the soup to taste with salt and pepper, then pour into serving bowls and garnish with the fried shallots and chives.

# Green Curry Noodle Soup
## with Mushrooms

*Serves 4*

Matcha lends its unique flavor to this creamy curry soup; not only does it stand up to the complex curry paste, but it enhances the dish with its verdant color. Feel free to customize the curry with any other mushrooms or herbs, such as cilantro or scallion greens, that you have on hand. The soup also makes a great vessel for adding odds-and-ends vegetables for a clean-out-the-fridge dish. If you want, you can swap the rice noodles for homemade matcha noodles; cut half the dough from the Matcha Pasta Dough recipe (page 118) into ⅛-inch-wide noodles, and cook them in the broth until tender, about 3 minutes.

2 tablespoons coconut oil

1 tablespoon Thai green curry paste, such as Thai Kitchen brand

1 tablespoon matcha, sifted

2 cups vegetable broth

Two 13.5-ounce cans unsweetened coconut milk

One 14-ounce package Asian rice noodles

14 ounces soft tofu, cut into 1-inch cubes

6 ounces shiitake or oyster mushrooms, thinly sliced

3½ ounces enoki mushrooms, roots trimmed

Kosher salt

1 cup mung bean sprouts

1 cup lightly packed basil leaves, preferably Thai basil

Heat the coconut oil in a large saucepan over medium heat. Add the curry paste and cook until fragrant and no longer raw, about 2 minutes. Stir in the matcha, then pour in the broth and coconut milk and bring to a boil.

Add the noodles to the simmering liquid and cook until al dente, about 2 minutes. Using a strainer, lift the noodles from the soup and transfer to 4 deep serving bowls.

Add the tofu and mushrooms to the soup and cook until just tender, about 2 minutes. Divide the tofu and mushrooms among the bowls. Season the soup with salt, and then ladle it into the bowls, top with the mung bean sprouts and basil, serve.

# Matcha Tempura
## with Matcha Mayonnaise

*Serves 6 to 8*

This tempura makes a great showcase for fresh green vegetables, which complement the flavor of the matcha in the batter, in the Matcha Salt (page 120) used for sprinkling, and in the matcha mayonnaise used for dipping. In addition to the vegetables listed below, which are the ones best shaped for dipping and eating like fries, you can also use cut broccoli or cauliflower florets, carrot sticks, or green beans. Don't make the matcha mayonnaise ahead of time; the matcha tends to congeal and separate from the mayonnaise if left to stand for over an hour.

Vegetable oil, for frying

3 cups all-purpose flour

2 tablespoons plus 1 teaspoon matcha, sifted

2 cups cold water plus ¼ cup ice cubes

2 egg yolks

2 pounds trimmed asparagus spears, broccolini, and sugar snap peas

Matcha Salt (page 120) and lemon wedges, for serving

½ cup mayonnaise, homemade or store-bought

Pour 2 inches of oil into a large Dutch oven and attach a deep-fry thermometer to the side. Heat the oil to 350°F over medium-high heat.

Meanwhile, whisk together 2 cups flour and 2 tablespoons matcha in a small bowl. In a large bowl, whisk the cold water and ice cubes with the egg yolks. Add the matcha flour and jab at it with the whisk (do not stir) until most of the flour is absorbed and forms a batter (there will be some small lumps left). Let the batter stand for 5 minutes.

Place the remaining 1 cup flour in a shallow bowl. Working in small batches, dredge the asparagus spears, broccolini, and sugar snap peas in the flour to coat; dip them in the batter; and then add them to the hot oil, stirring occasionally, until the vegetables are tender and the batter is golden brown and crisp, about 2 minutes.

Using a slotted spoon, lift the vegetables from the oil and transfer to paper towels to drain. Sprinkle them with Matcha Salt while hot.

In a small bowl, whisk the mayonnaise with the remaining 1 teaspoon matcha until smooth. Serve the tempura immediately with matcha mayonnaise and lemon wedges on the side.

# Matcha Pasta
## with Asparagus, Peas, and Ricotta

*Serves 2 to 4*

Asparagus and peas play off the green flavors of matcha in the homemade pasta dough, while ricotta adds dairy richness to the dish. This meal comes together in a matter of minutes, making it perfect for weeknight cooking. If you don't want to make the Matcha Pasta Dough, you can use an equal amount of store-bought fresh pasta (or 8 ounces of dried pasta) and stir 2 teaspoons of sifted matcha into the asparagus and peas before addingt them to the cooked pasta.

Kosher salt

½ recipe (10 ounces) Matcha Pasta Dough (page 118), cut into ⅜-inch-wide noodles

2 tablespoons unsalted butter

2 garlic cloves, finely chopped

1 cup fresh or frozen peas

½ bunch asparagus, trimmed and cut into 1½-inch lengths

Coarsely ground black pepper

8 ounces whole-milk ricotta

¼ teaspoon crushed red chile flakes

Bring a large pot of salted water to a boil. Add the pasta and cook, stirring occasionally, until al dente, about 3 to 4 minutes. Drain the pasta in a colander, reserving ½ cup of the pasta water.

Meanwhile, heat the butter in large nonstick skillet over medium-high heat. Add the garlic, stirring until lightly browned, about 1 minute. Add the peas and asparagus, stirring until just tender, about 3 minutes. Add the pasta and ¼ cup of the pasta water and toss to combine; add the remaining ¼ cup of pasta water if you want the pasta looser. Season the pasta with more salt and pepper.

Transfer the pasta to a serving plate, top with large spoonfuls of ricotta, and sprinkle with the chile flakes.

# Lamb Chops
## with Matcha-Mint Chimichurri

*Serves 4*

Matcha and mint are a perfect pairing in this floral take on the classic chimichurri sauce, the perfect condiment to serve alongside lean lamb chops. Make the chimichurri just before you're ready to serve it; matcha tends to darken and grow more bitter in flavor once it's mixed with the rest of the ingredients and exposed to air.

1½ cups packed mint leaves

½ cup packed flat-leaf parsley leaves

¼ cup packed cilantro leaves

¼ cup white wine vinegar

2 teaspoons matcha, sifted

2 teaspoons kosher salt, plus more

¼ teaspoon freshly ground white pepper

3 garlic cloves

½ jalapeño, stemmed

½ cup plus 2 tablespoons vegetable oil

12 lamb rib chops (about 1-inch thick)

In a food processor, combine the mint, parsley, cilantro, vinegar, matcha, 2 teaspoons salt, pepper, garlic, and jalapeño. While pulsing the food processor, drizzle in ½ cup oil until the mixture becomes a creamy yet slightly coarse sauce. Transfer the chimichurri sauce to a bowl, cover with plastic, and refrigerate for up to 1 hour.

Prepare a hot grill or heat a large cast-iron skillet over high heat. Season both sides of the lamb chops with salt, then drizzle with the remaining 2 tablespoons oil. Grill the chops (or sear in the skillet, working in batches), turning once halfway through, until golden brown on the outside and cooked to medium-rare inside, about 5 to 6 minutes total.

Transfer the lamb chops to a platter or plates and serve immediately with the chimichurri sauce.

# Chicken Poached in Matcha Broth
## with Lemongrass, Ginger, and Scallions

*Serves 4*

Matcha adds an earthy depth to this broth flavored with aromatic fresh ginger and lemongrass. The chicken can be poached up to a day ahead of time and then rewarmed in the broth, but in order to preserve the texture of the bok choy and cilantro, don't add them until just before you serve the dish. Aside from poaching, you can use this flavored broth (omit the chicken, bok choy, and cilantro) to make an even healthier version of chicken noodle soup; to cook grits, polenta, or oatmeal; or to sip on its own as a detoxifying tonic.

1 tablespoon vegetable oil

8 scallions, trimmed and cut into 3-inch lengths

One 3-inch piece ginger, peeled and cut into ¼-inch-thick slices

1 teaspoon matcha, sifted

6 cups chicken stock

1 lemongrass stalk

Kosher salt

4 boneless, skinless chicken breasts (about 6 ounces each)

4 baby bok choy, quartered (10 ounces total)

¼ cup cilantro leaves

Heat the oil in a large saucepan over medium heat. Add the scallions and ginger and cook to release the flavors and to soften slightly, about 2 minutes. Stir in the matcha, then pour in the stock and bring to a gentle simmer. Using the back of a knife or the end of a wooden spoon, bash the lemongrass stalk from end to end, tie the stalk into a knot, and add it to the pan. Season the broth to taste with salt.

Cut out a circle of parchment paper the diameter of the pan. Reduce the heat so the broth barely simmers, then add the chicken breasts. Cover the broth with the parchment paper, then cover the pan with its lid. Continue cooking, flipping the chicken breasts halfway through, until they're just cooked through, about 15 to 18 minutes.

Remove and discard the parchment and transfer the chicken to a cutting board. Add the bok choy to the broth and cook until just tender, about 4 to 6 minutes. Cut the chicken into thick slices and add to the broth along with the bok choy, scallions, and ginger. Divide among 4 bowls, top with cilantro leaves, and serve.

# Tuna Poké Bowl
## with Matcha Rice and Seaweed Salad

*Serves 4*

Matcha is a natural addition to Hawaiian poké, in which it mimics the seaweed traditionally mixed with raw tuna. With a foundation of matcha-infused rice, this poké bowl is packed with veggies, too, including cucumber, edamame, and avocado, and it's topped with a flavorful seaweed salad and a matcha and soy sauce dressing spiked with chile flakes.

1 cup short-grain rice

½ teaspoon kosher salt

1 tablespoon vegetable oil

2 teaspoons matcha, sifted

1 pound sushi-grade tuna, cut into ½-inch cubes

¼ cup soy sauce

1 tablespoon fresh lemon juice

1 tablespoon toasted sesame oil

1 teaspoon crushed red chile flakes

1 cup cooked edamame

1 avocado

½ cucumber, cut into ½-inch cubes

1 cup prepared seaweed salad, preferably wakame (available at Asian markets)

1 teaspoon toasted sesame seeds

One 4-by-4-inch sheet nori (toasted seaweed), cut into thin matchsticks (optional)

Make the matcha rice: Place the rice in a sieve and rinse under cold water until it runs clear. Place the rice in a medium saucepan, then add ½ teaspoon salt and 1½ cups water and bring to a boil. Reduce the heat to low, cover the pan, and cook undisturbed for 15 minutes. Meanwhile, stir the oil and 1 teaspoon matcha together into a slurry.

Remove the pan from the heat and let stand to steam the rice, about 10 minutes. Uncover the pan and stir in the matcha slurry. Scrape the rice onto a baking sheet and let cool to room temperature.

Combine the tuna, soy sauce, lemon juice, sesame oil, and chile flakes in a large bowl and toss to coat the tuna evenly with the dressing. Refrigerate the tuna for 10 minutes. Meanwhile, combine the edamame, avocado, and cucumber in another bowl and season with salt.

Divide the rice among 4 bowls and top with the edamame mixture and tuna. Divide the seaweed among the bowls and sprinkle the tuna with the sesame seeds and nori before serving.

# *Matcha Pasta Dough*

*Makes 1 ¼ pounds*

Matcha is an unorthodox ingredient in pasta dough, but its unique flavor shines through in noodles when they're combined with simple ingredients. By using a food processor, this dough comes together in seconds and doesn't require kneading. In addition to the Matcha Pasta with Asparagus, Peas, and Ricotta (page 110), use this fresh pasta in other simple pasta dishes: tossed with brown butter and sage, dotted with goat cheese, or tossed with a splash of cream and thinly shaved garlic.

3 cups all-purpose flour, plus more for tossing noodles

1½ tablespoons matcha, sifted

1 teaspoon salt

1 tablespoon vegetable oil

3 large eggs

1 large egg yolk

Combine the flour, matcha, and salt in a food processor and pulse to mix evenly. Add the oil, eggs, egg yolk, and 3 tablespoons lukewarm water and process until the dough gathers in a ball around the blade or bunches into a mass. Transfer the dough ball to a work surface and knead briefly into a smooth ball. Wrap the dough in plastic wrap and refrigerate for 1 hour.

Using a pasta machine (or rolling pin), divide the dough into quarters and pass each quarter through the pasta machine, starting with the widest setting and decreasing the setting after each roll, until you reach 1/16 inch (the next-to-last setting). Cut one sheet of dough in half crosswise and roll each half, starting with a short end, into a flat, 2-inch-wide log. Cut the log crosswise into ¼-inch noodles, transfer them to a baking sheet, and then sprinkle the noodles with flour and toss to separate them. Continue rolling and cutting the remaining three-quarters of pasta dough in the same manner.

If not using right away, wrap the entire baking sheet in plastic wrap and refrigerate the pasta for up to 2 days or freeze for up to 1 week.

To cook, drop the noodles into boiling salted water, stirring frequently until al dente, about 3 to 4 minutes (add 1 extra minute if cooking frozen dough). Drain the noodles and use in the Matcha Pasta with Asparagus, Peas, and Ricotta (page 110), or toss with your favorite sauce.

# Matcha Salt

*Makes 1 cup*

This salt is a great condiment for matcha lovers to keep handy so they can sprinkle their favorite ingredient on virtually everything they eat. In addition to seasoning the Matcha Tempura (page 108), you can sprinkle this salt on top of chocolate chip cookies, a seared ribeye steak, or a mix of crackers and nuts for a bar snack.

1 cup flaky sea salt

2 tablespoons matcha, sifted

Combine the salt and matcha in a bowl until evenly mixed. Transfer to a container and keep for up to 6 months.

# Chapter 6
# Matcha Mixology

## A Better Green Juice

Why not throw something healthy into a cocktail? It can't hurt!

Recipe developer Ben Mims says there is one key to mixing matcha cocktails, and that's to add matcha to a syrup (page 126) that can be blended into the drink. The syrup will keep in the refrigerator for several days, though it might start to turn brown after a day or two. It's important to not let a matcha-based cocktail sit around, otherwise it will start to darken and taste bitter. But seriously, who is letting a matcha cocktail sit around? Nobody puts matcha in the corner.

As far as different liquors go, matcha works best with gin and vodka (as do our dancing skills). Some folks like it with bourbon and sherry. However, matcha's sexy neon-green color requires dairy, which is rarely involved in cocktails. So if dairy isn't part of your matcha drink, the color can get kind of murky. If cocktail aesthetics are a concern, serve your matcha beverage in an opaque or colored glass.

And as we've mentioned before, not all matcha is made to be shaken and served cold. As one mixologist puts it, "The finer the grind, the easier it is to mix and shake." (A sentence that also gives us flashbacks to awkward eighth-grade dances.)

Add the matcha drinks that follow–boozy and non-alcoholic alike–to your repetoire for when you want something more than a shot or latte.

# Alcoholic Drinks

## Sake-to-Me Cocktail

*Serves 1*

This cocktail, popular in the Little Tokyo neighborhood of Los Angeles, is the simplest non-dairy way to enjoy matcha every day. It's a low-maintenance and low-proof tonic, perfect for large parties because you can make it in large batches and continuously dole it out as your guests guzzle it down.

**1 teaspoon matcha, sifted**

**2 ounces sake**

**Dash fresh lime juice**

Combine all the ingredients in a cocktail shaker with ½ cup lukewarm water and stir. Fill the shaker with crushed ice and shake for 10 seconds. Strain into an ice-filled highball glass (or serve neat in a coupe) and serve.

# Matcha Old-Fashioned

*Serves 1*

Matcha's bitterness plays off the caramel notes of whiskey and the sweetness of muddled orange and brandied cherry in this classic cocktail. If you don't have Matcha Cocktail Syrup on hand, substitute with 1 teaspoon of simple syrup and ¼ teaspoon of sifted matcha.

1 orange wheel

½ ounce club soda

1 teaspoon Matcha Cocktail Syrup (see below)

4 dashes Angostura bitters

2 ounces Japanese whiskey

1 brandied cherry, for garnish

1 orange twist, for garnish

In a rocks glass, muddle 1 orange wheel with the soda, syrup, and bitters until the rind falls off. Discard the rind, add the whiskey, and fill the glass with ice. Garnish with the cherry and orange twist and serve.

# Matcha Cocktail Syrup

*Makes about 6 tablespoons (3 ounces)*

This all-purpose matcha syrup is a great addition to your bar. Keep it handy for adding to cocktails, mixing with soda water for a refreshing tonic, or drizzling over fruit salad or oatmeal for breakfast. Because matcha tends to turn darker and more bitter after it's heated, use this syrup within 3 days, and keep it refrigerated and sealed in an airtight container the whole time to preserve its flavor and color.

⅓ cup granulated sugar

1 tablespoon matcha, sifted

Combine the sugar, matcha, and ¼ cup water in a small saucepan and bring to barely a simmer, stirring occasionally, until the sugar dissolves. Pour into an airtight container or squeeze bottle and refrigerate for up to 3 days.

# Harajuku Gimlet

*Serves 1*

In this riff on the classic gin cocktail from Cafe Clover in New York City, the subtle floral flavor of shiso leaves finds a match in matcha. The matcha is mixed into a simple syrup made with fragrant, slightly bitter yuzu juice. As with the Matcha Cocktail Syrup (page 126), make the Yuzu-Matcha Mix just before making the cocktail, and use it within 3 days to keep the matcha from turning dark or becoming more bitter.

2 fresh shiso leaves (available at Asian markets)

1½ ounces dry gin, preferably Tanqueray No. 10 or Portobello Road brand

1½ ounces Yuzu-Matcha Mix (recipe follows)

Lemon and lime wheels and orange twist, for garnish

Combine 1 shiso leaf, the gin, and the Yuzu-Matcha Mix in an ice-filled cocktail shaker. Shake until chilled, then strain into a chilled coupe or martini glass. Garnish with the remaining shiso leaf, lemon and lime wheels, and the orange twist and serve.

*Yuzu-Matcha Mix: Combine ¼ cup simple syrup, ¼ cup yuzu juice, and 1½ teaspoons sifted matcha in a small saucepan. Heat over medium heat until fragrant, then remove from the heat and let cool completely. Transfer to a resealable container and refrigerate for up to 3 days.*

## Ask the Expert:

*How I came up with my signature matcha drink:*

I went into this whole Japanese world and wanted to see what ingredients I could use with matcha that would make sense. I decided to do an irreverent spin on a gimlet. I muddled shiso with the Tanqueray No. 10 gin and then pureed the matcha with the yuzu instead of using lime juice. The matcha gave it earthiness and pop of green. I called it the Harajuku Gimlet.

*Matcha obstacles:*

The hardest thing was to get the matcha to infuse properly. I put the powder into the yuzu and use a blender to whip all together. There's a really simple syrup that I added into that. So the infusion of the matcha and simple syrup became nice and smooth.

*Johnny Swet*
*Consulting mixologist, Cafe Clover,*
*New York City*

# Matcha Mint Julep

*Serves 1*

The natural pairing of matcha and mint makes the tea stand out in a classic mint julep. Dusting the top of the drink with matchafied confectioners' sugar is an optional (but highly recommended) flourish.

¼ cup packed fresh mint leaves, plus more for garnish

1 tablespoon granulated sugar

1¼ teaspoons matcha, sifted

2 ounces bourbon

1 teaspoon fresh lemon juice

1 tablespoon confectioners' sugar

Combine the mint, sugar, and 1 teaspoon matcha in a cocktail shaker and gently muddle until the sugar has dissolved (don't tear the mint). Add 3 ounces of water and the bourbon and lemon juice and stir to combine. Fill the shaker with ice, stir until chilled, strain into a julep or rocks glass filled with crushed ice, and garnish with a mint bouquet.

Mix the remaining ¼ teaspoon matcha with the confectioners' sugar and dust the top of the cocktail before serving.

# Matcha Bloody Mary

*Serves 1*

Matcha enhances the other vegetal flavors in this verdant take on the classic Bloody Mary made with green tomatoes, cucumbers, and chiles. Packing each glass with pickled green vegetables, such as green beans, cornichons, okra, or green olives, makes the drink a meal in itself. Feel free to use gin, tequila, or mezcal in place of vodka; all of these spirits work well with the floral flavors of matcha.

1½ ounces vodka

1 teaspoon matcha, sifted

¼ teaspoon kosher salt

2 small to medium green tomatoes

1 sprig each cilantro and flat-leaf parsley, plus more for garnish

½ small cucumber

½ serrano chile, stemmed and seeded

1 lime wedge, for garnish

Assorted pickled vegetables, for garnish

Combine all the ingredients except for the lime wedge and pickled vegetables in a blender and puree until smooth. Pour into an ice-filled glass and garnish with a lime wedge, cilantro and parsley sprigs, and any pickled vegetables you have, such as green beans, okra, green olives, cornichons, and pearl onions.

# Time Out of Mind

*Serves 1*

Inspired by the strong, fruity aroma of matcha, this cocktail from The Up & Up in Manhattan uses bourbon, crème de cacao, and beer to stand up to the strong flavor of the tea. Instead of being tasked to create a smooth or elegant cocktail, the ingredients in this drink exist to intensify the assertive flavors of matcha. Serve it at the end of a meal, as it can stand in as both dessert and digestif.

1½ ounces rye whiskey, preferably Virgil Kaine High-Rye Bourbon

1 ounce crème de cacao

½ ounce PX sherry

½ ounce fresh lemon juice

½ teaspoon matcha, sifted

4 to 6 ounces lager beer

Combine all the ingredients except the beer in an ice-filled cocktail shaker and shake until chilled, about 10 seconds. Strain into an ice-filled highball glass, top with the beer and serve.

# Matcha Royale

*Serves 1*

Although this simple Champagne cocktail won't win any beauty contests, it highlights the Matcha Cocktail Syrup better than any other alcoholic drink. Be sure to make the syrup just before serving to keep the matcha's bright-green color intact.

2 teaspoons Matcha Cocktail Syrup (page 126)

Chilled Champagne or prosecco

Pour the syrup into a chilled Champagne flute or coupe, top with Champagne, and serve.

# Matcha-Hopper

*Serves 1*

Whereas crème de menthe adds a toxic green hue to the grasshopper cocktail, matcha lends a natural color as well as light bitterness to balance the sweet ice cream and crème de cacao for this adult milkshake that may or may not be good for you.

1 cup vanilla ice cream

½ cup whole milk

1 ounce crème de cacao

1 tablespoon matcha, sifted

½ ounce Matcha Cocktail Syrup
(page 126)

Combine the ice cream, milk, crème de cacao, and matcha in a blender and puree until smooth. Pour into a chilled glass, drizzle with the Matcha Cocktail Syrup and serve.

# Matcha Mojito

*Serves 1*

This whimsical take on the classic Cuban cocktail, from The Little Beet Table in New York City and Chicago, utilizes silver rum because its mellow sugarcane flavor and notes of banana, citrus, and peppermint balance the earthiness of the matcha.

5 mint leaves, plus more for garnish

3 lime wedges

1½ ounces silver rum, preferably Mount Gay

½ ounce lime juice

½ ounce agave syrup or simple syrup

½ teaspoon matcha, sifted

1 ounce soda water

Combine the mint leaves and lime wedges in a cocktail shaker and muddle until fragrant. Add the rum, lime juice, syrup, and matcha. Fill the shaker with ice and shake until well chilled. Strain into an ice-filled rocks glass, top with the soda, garnish with more mint, and serve.

## Ask the Expert:

*How I came up with my signature matcha drink:*

I've always been a tea drinker. When we opened Little Beet Table, we carried In Pursuit of Tea and I had a meeting with the brand's owner, because I really wanted to start incorporating tea into some cocktails. He was like, "You should think about matcha. We do have an iced matcha that you can shake and pour over ice." I was blown away. It's earthy and bittersweet, a little vegetal. It was amazing. I started to think about what this would be great with. I thought, everyone likes a mojito. The sugarcaney rum would enhance the vegetal flavor, which the citrus would cut through. So the Matcha Mojito was born.

*Matcha obstacles:*

Not all matcha is made to be shaken and served cold. Look for a finer grind.

*Jenifer Cerio*
*Director of operations, The Little Beet Table, New York City*

# Matcha, Coconut Milk, and Mezcal Frozen Punch

*Serves 4*

In this tropical, creamy punch, the coconut milk, floral edge of the grapefruit juice, and smoky mezcal tame the matcha. This is a great drink for an outdoor barbecue or taco spread, and it's an easy one to multiply to serve more people. (The grapefruit sugar used to rim the glasses is also great for margaritas, salty dogs, sidecars, or to sprinkle over a lemon pound cake or sugar cookies.)

1²/₃ cups unsweetened coconut milk

½ cup mezcal

½ cup fresh grapefruit juice, plus 1 tablespoon finely grated grapefruit zest

¼ cup fresh lemon juice

¼ cup turbinado, light muscovado, or light brown sugar

2 tablespoons matcha, sifted

¼ cup granulated sugar

Coconut chunks and grapefruit twists, for garnish

Combine the coconut milk, mezcal, grapefruit juice, lemon juice, turbinado, matcha, and 4 cups of ice cubes in a blender and puree until smooth.

In a small dish, rub the grapefruit zest with the granulated sugar until lightly colored and evenly combined. Freeze 4 glasses for 5 minutes. Remove the glasses from the freezer, dip the rims in the matcha sugar and zest, and let stand for 1 minute.

Fill the glasses with punch, garnish with coconut chunks and grapefruit twists, and serve.

# Matcha Tea Party

*Serves 1*

Matcha balances the sweet elderflower liqueur and white rum in this refreshing summer-time cocktail, which was inspired by a punch infused with green tea bags.

2 ounces white rum

1 ounce dry vermouth

1 ounce water

2½ teaspoons St-Germain elderflower liqueur

1 teaspoon matcha, sifted

Dash Angostura bitters

Lime twist, for garnish

Combine all ingredients except the lime twist in an ice-filled cocktail shaker and shake until chilled, about 15 seconds. Strain into an ice-filled glass, garnish with the lime twist and serve.

# Matcha G&T

*Serves 1*

Matcha and club soda stand in for tonic water's bitterness in this classic cocktail, in which the floral botanicals in the gin also enhance the aroma of the matcha.

2 ounces dry gin

6 ounces soda water

½ ounce Matcha Cocktail Syrup (page 126)

Lime and lemon wedges, for garnish

Pour the gin in a highball glass, top with ice, and then add the soda water. Top with the matcha syrup, garnish with lime and lemon wedges, and serve.

# Matcha Dark and Stormy

*Serves 1*

Rum and ginger, with their affinity for sweet flavors, pair perfectly in this spin on the dark and stormy. Use the best ginger beer–such as Boylan, Gosling's, or Reed's–you can find.

1 ounce white rum

1 ounce dark rum

1 tablespoon Matcha Cocktail Syrup (page 126)

8 ounces ginger beer

Lime wedge to garnish

Combine both rums and the syrup in a highball glass and fill with ice. Top with the ginger beer, stir once or twice, garnish with the lime wedge, and serve.

# Matcha Pimm's Cup

*Serves 1*

Sweet Pimm's liqueur and fruit are a perfect match for matcha in this cocktail. For a very different twist on sangria, substitute the soda water with prosecco.

⅛ small cucumber, thinly sliced

2 strawberries, thinly sliced

⅛ orange, thinly sliced

⅛ lemon, thinly sliced

⅛ green apple, thinly sliced

2 ounces Pimm's Cup No. 1

6 ounces soda water

2 teaspoons Matcha Cocktail Syrup (page 126)

Mint sprigs, for garnish

Combine the cucumber, strawberries, orange, lemon, and apple in a highball glass, top with ice, and pour in the Pimm's. Combine the soda water and syrup in a glass and then pour into the fruit-filled highball glass. Garnish with mint and serve.

# Matcha Slushy

*Serves 4*

This refreshing frozen cocktail, from The Skylark in Manhattan, amps up the flavor of matcha with brewed green tea. Serve this adult lemonade straight from the blender with plenty of fresh lemon wheels for a relaxed backyard party.

8 ounces vodka, preferably Tito's

6 ounces fresh lemon juice

6 ounces honey

6 ounces brewed green tea (regular green tea, not matcha)

1 tablespoon matcha

Lemon wheels, for garnish

Blend all ingredients (except the lemon wheels) with ice in a blender until smooth. Pour into glasses, garnish with lemon wheels, and serve.

# Non-Alcoholic Drinks

## Citrus, Matcha, and Sour-Plum Ade

*Serves 4*

Matcha balances the salty-sweet dried plums and bright citrus in this refreshing drink. Double or triple this recipe and let the fruit hang out in the water for up to 1 week, if you like.

2 regular limes or 6 key limes

1 Cara Cara or navel orange

10 dried sour plums (available at an Asian market)

¼ cup honey

2 teaspoons matcha, sifted

Cut each lime and orange into 8 wedges (or halve the key limes) and squeeze their juice into a pitcher. Add the spent wedges and plums and 5 cups water. Let the ade sit in the refrigerator for at least 24 hours to allow the fruit to infuse the water.

For each drink, place 1 tablespoon honey and ½ teaspoon matcha in a cocktail shaker and fill with 1 cup of the citrus ade. Shake vigorously to dissolve the honey and matcha, then strain the mixture into a glass filled with ice. Serve with a couple of pieces of the macerated fruit in the glass.

# Matcha Lemonade

*Serves 4*

Matcha's earthy, floral taste adds complexity to summertime's classic tart lemonade. To make a Matcha Arnold Palmer, see the recipe below.

1½ cups fresh lemon juice
(about 6 lemons)

1 cup granulated sugar

2 teaspoons matcha, sifted

Whisk together the lemon juice, sugar, matcha, and 4 cups water in a bowl until the sugar dissolves. Strain the lemonade into a pitcher and pour over ice to serve.

*To make a Matcha Arnold Palmer, bring 5 cups water to a boil in a medium saucepan, then remove from the heat and add 3 black tea bags; let brew for 20 minutes. Remove and discard the tea bags and mix the tea with 1 recipe of Matcha Lemonade in a large pitcher. Refrigerate until chilled and serve over ice.*

# *Hot Matcha and White Chocolate*

*Serves 8*

This festive and fragrant alternative to traditional hot chocolate is essentially a matcha latte sweetened with white chocolate. Use the highest-quality white chocolate you can find, since others will contain an overpowering amount of vanilla, which will detract from the flavor of the matcha.

4 cups whole milk

2 cups heavy cream

2 tablespoons matcha, sifted

½ teaspoon kosher salt

8 ounces white chocolate, chopped

Combine the milk, cream, matcha, and salt in a large saucepan and bring to a simmer, whisking constantly. Remove from the heat, add the white chocolate, and let stand for 1 minute. Whisk the mixture until smooth, then pour into warm mugs and serve.

# Caribbean Matcha, Date, and Cashew Smoothie

## Serves 4

Raw cashews thicken and enrich this tropical smoothie without dairy fat, while dates add enough sweetness to balance the earthy matcha. For a thinner drink, blend all the ingredients without ice and then serve the drink over ice.

2½ cups sugarcane juice or maple water (or ½ cup agave nectar mixed with 2 cups water)

1 cup raw cashews

½ cup pitted dates

2 teaspoons matcha, sifted

One ½-inch piece of peeled and sliced ginger, coarsely chopped

Combine all the ingredients in a blender with 2 cups of ice and puree until very smooth, at least 1 minute. Pour into glasses and serve.

# Matcha Lassi

*Serves 1*

With its cooling yogurt richness, the classic lassi provides the perfect canvas for matcha. You can use coconut or soy yogurt and milk to make this drink vegan friendly.

1 cup plain, full-fat yogurt (not Greek)

¼ cup whole milk

2 tablespoons granulated sugar

2 teaspoons matcha, sifted

¼ teaspoon vanilla extract

Combine all the ingredients and ½ cup ice cubes in a blender and puree until smooth. Pour into a chilled glass to serve.

# Matcha Horchata

*Serves 1*

The richness of ground rice in this classic Mexican drink adds enough body to the sweetened dairy to balance the matcha, giving it extra depth in this otherwise simple preparation.

2 tablespoons medium or long-grain rice

1 tablespoon matcha, sifted, plus more for garnish

3 ounces evaporated milk

3½ ounces sweetened condensed milk

Toast the rice in a small skillet over medium heat until it smells nutty, about 1 to 2 minutes. Remove from the heat, transfer to a blender with the matcha, and blend into a fine powder. Add both milks and 1 cup water and puree until evenly combined.

Strain through a fine sieve into a bowl and refrigerate until chilled, at least 1 hour. Pour into two ice-filled glasses and dust with more matcha right before serving.

# Matcha Thai Iced Tea

*Serves 6*

In traditional Thai preparation, cream and sweetened condensed milk are mixed into tea, and this method lends itself exceptionally well to matcha. The sweet dairy mellows the matcha's earthy qualities.

4 tablespoons matcha, sifted

¾ cup granulated sugar

6 tablespoons sweetened condensed milk

6 tablespoons heavy cream

Whisk together the matcha and sugar in a bowl, then stir in 1 cup boiling water and stir until the sugar dissolves. Pour in 5 cups cold water and refrigerate until ready to serve.

To serve, stir the sweetened condensed milk and cream together in a bowl until smooth. Pour the tea into 6 tall ice-filled glasses, add 2 tablespoons of the milk-cream mixture to each glass, and stir to combine.

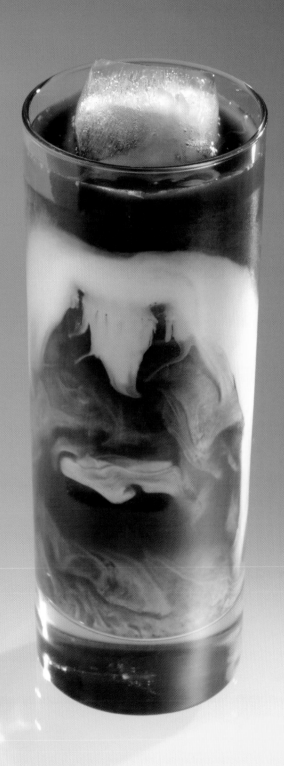

# Matchapedia

**Americano:** A matcha shot added to about 8 to 12 ounces of hot water.

**Camellia sinensis:** All teas come from this plant.

**Cappuccino:** One part matcha shot, one part steamed milk, one part foam.

**Ceremonial grade:** The highest-quality matcha made using only the newest and greenest top two buds of the plant. Processed and ground by traditional standards. Best drunk as a ceremonial shot.

**Ceremonial shot:** 2 grams of high-grade matcha blended or whisked with 2 ounces of hot water. This is the "shot" building block in many matcha drinks.

**Chanoyu:** The traditional Japanese tea ceremony.

**Chasen:** A bamboo tea whisk used to mix the powdered tea with hot water.

**Chashaku:** A bamboo tea scoop used to scoop tea from the tea caddy into the tea bowl.

**Chawan:** A tea bowl available in a wide range of sizes, styles, and prices.

**Cortado:** A matcha shot with less milk than a latte, but more milk than a macchiato.

**Crema:** A foam that forms on the top of freshly made matcha.

**Culinary grade:** Lower-quality matcha made from older and darker leaves or produced by machinery. Best used in milk-based drinks, baking, and cooking. Should not be drunk as a shot.

**DEFCON matcha:** 10 grams of matcha mixed with minimal water. May help you take over the world.

**Dirty matcha:** A shot of espresso combined with a matcha drink.

**Everyday grade:** A lower-level ceremonial grade using leaves lower down on the plant.

**Free-form latte art:** Designs created on the top of milk-based drinks using only a pitcher and milk. Most common designs are the rosette, tulip, and heart.

**Fukuoka:** The capital city of Fukuoka Prefecture, which is situated on the northern shore of the island of Kyushu in Japan. An up-and-coming producer of matcha.

**Hishaku:** A long bamboo ladle used to transfer hot water from the *kama* to the tea bowl.

**Iced latte:** A matcha shot served with cold milk over ice.

**Iced tea:** A matcha Americano served over ice.

**Kama:** An iron or copper pot used to heat up water.

**Koicha:** Thick tea. Usually prepared with a higher matcha to water ratio.

**Latte:** A matcha shot with steamed milk.

**L-theanine:** An amino acid found in high quantities in matcha believed to reduce mental and physical stress, improve cognition, and boost mood and cognitive performance in a synergistic manner with caffeine.

**Macchiato:** A matcha shot with a little bit of steamed milk.

**Matcha:** Shade-grown and powdered green tea. The only suspension tea in the Japanese tea canon.

**Matcharista:** The lovely person behind the counter that makes delicious matcha drinks.

**Matcha stain:** The green residue left on lips and teeth after consuming a matcha beverage.

**Natsume:** The small lidded container or tea caddy in which powdered tea is placed.

**Nishio:** A city located in Aichi Prefecture, in the Chūbu region of Japan. It is a regional commercial and manufacturing center and the country's leading producer of matcha in terms of volume.

**Satori:** A calm euphoria.

**Sencha:** Sun-grown and steeped green tea. The most popular tea produced in Japan.

**Suspension tea:** Tea that does not dissolve in water. The ground leaves are whisked into the water and suspended, versus being steeped or brewed.

**Tea master:** Someone who makes, boils, infuses, and serves tea; in other words, a server in a teahouse.

**Uji:** A city on the southern outskirts of the city of Kyoto, in Kyoto Prefecture, Japan. The most well-known hub of matcha production.

**Umami:** A savory taste. One of the five basic tastes along with sweetness, sourness, bitterness, and saltiness.

**Usucha:** Thin tea, usually prepared with equal amounts matcha and water.

**Viscosity:** The state of being thick, sticky, and semifluid in consistency due to internal friction.

# Resources

## Jessica and Anna's Favorite Brands and Matcha Bars

Alfred Tea Room—Los Angeles, CA

alfredtea.com

Breakaway Matcha—San Anselmo, CA

breakawaymatcha.com

Café Integral—New York, NY

cafeintegral.com

Cha Cha Matcha—New York, NY

chachamatcha.com

Chailait—New York, NY

chalait.com

Erewhon—Los Angeles, CA

erewhonmarket.com

In Pursuit of Tea—New York, NY

inpursuitoftea.com

Ippodo Tea—Kyoto, Japan, and New York, NY

ippodo-tea.co.jp/en/shop/ny.html

Kettl—Brooklyn, NY

kettl.co

MatchaBar—New York, NY

matchabarnyc.com

Matcha Cafe Wabi—New York, NY

facebook.com/Matcha-Cafe-Wabi-456245654478852/

Matcha Maiden—South Melbourne, Victoria, Australia

matchamaidenusa.myshopify.com

Matcha Source/Matcha Box—Los Angeles, CA

matchasource.com

Samovar Tea Bar—San Francisco, CA

samovartea.com

Toby's Estate—New York, NY (for latte art classes)

tobysestate.com

## Drinks, Pastries and More

Café Clover—New York, NY

cafeclovernyc.com

Jen Yee Pastry—New York, NY

jenyeepastry.com

The Little Beet Table—New York, NY, and Chicago, IL

thelittlebeettable.com

Valerie Confections—Los Angeles, CA

valerieconfections.com

## Traditional Tea Ceremony

Keiko Kitazawa-Koch-New York, NY

murasakinj.exblog.jp

# *Index*

# Acknowledgments

To our matcha connoisseurs who went above and beyond to help us with this book, especially Ippodo Tea Co., Eric Gower, Jesse Jacobs, Matthew Morton, and Michelle Puyane—our sincerest thanks. And thanks also to matcha lovers Jenifer Cerio, Kathy YL Chan, Valerie Gordon, Sarah Holloway, Zach Mangan, Mathew Rice, Kristin Surak, Johnny Swet, Alissa White, and Jen Yee. Your insights were invaluable.

To our anonymous matcharistas—you know who you are. Thanks for pretending not to listen in on our conversations and judge us when we sit at the bar on Saturdays talking about how hard it is to find a good protein powder and whether or not we should get gold or black Nike Dunk Sky Hi's (spoiler alert...we got both).

To our family, friends, and bosses for your continued support during this project—yes, it is possible for two people to talk this much about matcha.

And to Dovetail publisher and editor Nick Fauchald. We are your biggest fans.

Cheers! Or, as one might say in Japanese, *kanpai*!

# About the Authors

## Anna Kavaliunas

is a marketing executive who was worked in the entertainment industry on both coasts for twelve years. She has also consulted for companies in the health and wellness industry and has published articles on the subject. She's an avid adventure traveler, a certified yoga instructor, and is pretty sure her blood has turned green from her current matcha obsession.

## Jessica Flint

is a New York–based editor and writer who has held staff positions at *Vanity Fair*, *Bloomberg Businessweek*, *Marie Claire*, and *Departures*, where she is currently a senior features editor overseeing travel, food, and beverage coverage. In 2016, she spent fifteen days traveling throughout Japan, and learned about matcha by attending tea ceremonies, traveling to tea houses, and staying overnight in *ryokans* and Buddhist temples.

Published by Dovetail Press in Brooklyn, New York, a division of Assembly Brands LLC.

For details or ordering information, contact the publisher at the address below or email **info@dovetail.press.**

Dovetail Press
42 West Street #403
Brooklyn, NY 11222
**www.dovetail.press**

Library of Congress Cataloging-in-Publication data is on file with the publisher.

ISBN: 978-0-9898882-6-4

First Edition

Printed in the United States

10 9 8 7 6 5 4 3 2 1